AF344845

Quantum Computing

Mastering in 60 minutes

Franck FRANCHIN

First Edition (in French): June 2019
Original Title: « Informatique Quantique : 60 min pour comprendre »

First Edition (in English): July 2019

ISBN-13 : 978-2-97007112-9 (ebook)
ISBN-13 : 978-2-97007113-6 (print)

DEDICATION

to Mr. Jacques BOUCHER,
my teacher of semiconductor physics at ENSEEIHT
who managed to make me like Mathematics
to better understand Physics.

TABLE OF CONTENTS

ACKNOWLEDGEMENTS

Charles Beigbeder, Dr. Alessandro Curioni, Gaëlle Dussutour,
Alina Yasynenko

WELCOME TO THE QUANTUM AGE

"Electrons are particles. Light is a wave." For too long, this incomplete view of nature has stifled our imaginations and constrained what we think we can do with technology. But that's about to change.

Classical computing has served society incredibly well. It gave us the Internet and cashless commerce. It sent men to the moon, put robots on Mars and smartphones in our pockets. But many of the world's biggest mysteries and potentially greatest opportunities remain beyond the grasp of classical computers. To continue the pace of progress, we need to augment the classical approach with a new platform, one that follows its own set of rules.

It's called Quantum Computing.

Quantum computers are incredibly powerful machines that take a new approach to processing information. Built on the principles of quantum mechanics, they exploit complex and fascinating laws of nature that are always there, but usually remain hidden from view. By harnessing such natural behavior, quantum computers can run new types of algorithms to process information more holistically. They may one day lead to revolutionary breakthroughs in materials and drug discovery, the optimization of complex manmade systems, such as supply chains and financial risk, and artificial intelligence.

We expect them to open doors that we once thought would remain locked indefinitely.

Imagine you could travel back in time to better prepare yourself for the rise of the Internet or mobile phones. That's the opportunity that exists now with quantum computing. This is why IBM has put the world's first quantum computer in the cloud, for anyone to use and why we formed IBM Q, the industry's first commercial program to build a universal quantum computer.

The goal is to make sure that everyone from students to CEOs to become *"quantum ready"*.

At IBM we find the prospect of exploring the full capabilities of quantum computing to be incredibly exciting. And we hope you do, too.

Dr. Alessandro Curioni
IBM Fellow, Vice-President, Europe and
IBM Research Director - Zurich

PREFACE

Quantum Mechanics was born during the extraordinary decade 1920-1930. Almost a century ago, giant thinkers theorized the behavior of matter on the atomic scale, and their theories were confirmed by experimentation. Almost all our modern world is indebted to them: atomic fission, transistor then laser, hard drive, in short all that builds our nowadays electronics and thus our whole digital society.

At theoretical level, these early glorious times were followed by a kind of "quantum winter" during which physicists, probably troubled by the Bohr-Einstein controversy over the possible incompleteness of quantum mechanics, did not seek to delve deeper into the consequences of this new physics on the behavior of particles as individual entities.

It was not until the 80s that the famous experiments of the French physicist Alain Aspect, based on the work of his Irish colleague John Bell, settle the question and confirm the strange properties of individual particles arising from quantum theory: superposition and entanglement.

So the humanity entered into the second quantum revolution! Of which we still only perceive the foam of the coming waves.

In metrology and imaging, applications have quick wins. Based on single-particle interferometry, new quantum sensors have been imagined. They are extremely efficient, for many already operational. They measure certain quantities such as magnetic fields (new MRI), accelerations (new gravimeters and gyroscopes), gaining several orders of magnitude. A promising project plans to take advantage of quantum fluctuations of single photons to increase the sensitivity of Ligo and Virgo (gravitational wave recorders).

Encryption is another short-term application area. The linear feature of the superposition and the super-correlation offered by entanglement forbid any identical replication of a qubit. The qubit becomes a new vector of information, infinitely richer than the binary bit, thus making it possible to perfectly secure any data transmission..

China has also decided to make the leap forward of quantum cryptography and invests heavily in the construction of a quantum communication network linking its strategic centers. Everywhere on the planet, you can observe a veritable boiling of scientific publications and new business incorporations related to these new technologies of encryption. The NSA, the ANSSI and their worldwide equivalents have all reviewed their security protocols. And Europe could soon build a Quantum Internet Network too!

Finally, of course, high performance computing (HPC) is a hot candidate for quantum computing. It is the combination of the superposition principle and the entanglement property that makes it possible to design new algorithms to solve the most complex problems because they can be performed simultaneously. Admittedly, for large-scale implementation, progress must be made in the manipulation of individual quantum objects in order to limit the loss of purely quantum qualities. But the big news is that we have gone from the stage of scientific validation to the time of engineering and industrialization of products, the creation of start-ups, the filing of patents, the search for customers and talent recruitment.

Franck Franchin, I first met during my debut as an entrepreneur, passionate about this revolution, makes us discover this new world with pedagogy and realism, without yielding to the easy temptation of the utopian dream while drawing the vertiginous perspectives of these new technologies.

Charles Beigbeder
Quantonation Founder

INTRODUCTION

This book is the follow-up and companion of the eponymous conferences that I have given in France and in Switzerland for a few years. It is also the fruit of the remarks, criticisms and encouragements of those I had the pleasure of meeting during these 60 minutes sessions, with dynamic and rewarding exchanges.

It is intended for all of you who are interested in Quantum Computing and who want to understand the issues, in a synthetic and didactic way, without having to plunge into courses of linear algebra or fundamental physics. By the way, Quantum Physics and Quantum Mechanics are born thanks to Mathematics.

For those of you who feel comfortable with these complex mathematical concepts and who really want to understand why and how Quantum Computing, it's not the right book. I give several references of excellent works in the Bibliography section. For the most volunteers and quantum fans of you, I do recommend the academic reference on the subject, written by Michael Nielsen and Isaac Chuang [1].

The following chapters will introduce you to this new paradigm through deliberately marked paths.

Some may find that my wording is simple, even simplistic and sometimes slightly erroneous compared to the scientific reality. It is a choice that I assume in a spirit of popularization. Please remember all the pleasure you might have had by reading *"Popular Mechanics Magazine"* in your teens.

Chapters can be read in any order, although I recommend a linear reading. At the end of each Chapter, you can find a Summary that focuses on the key points addressed within the Chapter. From time to time, an inset deals with a particular topic, which is not essential to the full understanding of the concepts of the Chapter.

The book ends with a technical appendix that allows the most reckless of you to acquire the mathematical foundations of Quantum Computing.

I founded VoltaNode, a French-Swiss technology and innovation consulting company that works mainly with investors, venture capitalists, incubators and big name companies. We cover topics like IoT, Cybersecurity, Artificial Intelligence and Quantum Computing, of course.

We started working on Quantum topics almost ten years ago, mainly on aspects related to Cybersecurity (Cryptography and Quantum Internet). Since 2010, quantum stuff has got motion: community, simulators, tools, technological barriers breakers. Although there are still a lot of work to be done and some technological leaps to accomplish, all stakeholders are confident in this positive dynamic move.

In the following chapters, I will try to demystify Quantum Computing, giving to you the keys to understanding this new technological breakthrough and assessing its potential impact on your company, your suppliers and your customers.

Quantum Computing gossip is a bit like sex explained by teens. Many of them talk about it, but few have an actual practical experience.

Please let me quote Mr. Thierry Breton, CEO of Atos, a French company heavily involved in Quantum Computing. He uses the following metaphor to explain the *quantum effect*. Consider a room full of a thousand people. You have to find a 6-feet person who speaks French. With Traditional Computing, you have to interview each person one by one to know whether he is 6 feet tall and speaks French. It is a long and cumbersome process. In Quantum Computing, everything happens as if you speak with a megaphone : « *Please, can all people taller than 6 feet and speaking French raise their hand?* ». You get the answer almost instantly. Thierry Breton calls this type of computing *holistic* rather than *sequential*.

Some people say that this new technology will soon change the world, others temperate by stating that applications are currently extremely limited. My (current) vision is between these two points of view and I will try to share this feeling throughout the following chapters.

Remember the very first step of Man on the Moon. At the end of a frantic, political and technological race between the USSR and the United States, the latter, which had however fallen behind, managed to achieve this feat for Humanity. The technological challenges were huge: the Saturn V launcher, the mandatory protections against radiations and meteorites, the thrusters that were supposed to operate at 3,300°C, the space suits, not to mention the computing resources, which were very well limited at those times. I also remember the control room where engineers were standing in front of their screens (TV screen, no computer!), using their slide rules. Yet, 50 years later, this great scientific adventure still has daily impacts on our lives.

The pioneers of Quantum Computing face the same kinds of technological challenges. For the quantum noob and newbie, it is difficult to grasp this transdisciplinary complexity: mathematics, quantum physics, particle physics, physics of matter, chemistry, metallurgy, crystallography, cryogenics, mechanics and, of course, computer science. The level of expertise in each domain has to be very high, but, much more complicated, each stakeholder must understand the work of the others because the solutions are often transdisciplinary.

So, please take a seat and, as in Star Trek, let me take you on *"the Road to the Unknown…"*.

1. QUANTUM LOLCAT

It all started with a cat affairs, a kind of LOLCAT.

The furball in question is the cat of Mr. Erwin Schrödinger, illustrious Austrian physicist and one of the founding fathers of Quantum Mechanics.

Beware to sensible souls: an animal may be injured or killed in the remainder of this chapter.

Schrödinger imagined the following experiment: If a cat is placed in a sealed and opaque box with a Machiavellian system that has a 50% chance of killing the cat in the next 60 minutes, what will be the status of the cat at the end of this time?

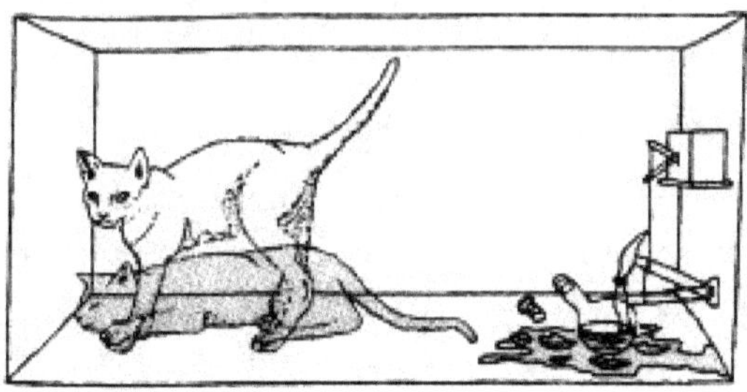

Figure 1: Schrödinger's cat experience

The first, most intuitive approach brings us to say that the cat will be either dead or alive.

But according to the principles of Quantum Physics, just before the moment the box is opened to check, the cat is *both* alive *and* dead, at the same time!

The cat's condition is actually defined only when the box is really opened: alive *or* dead. Before opening the box, the condition of the cat is only a probability: 50% alive *and* 50% dead.

This principle is called the **superposition** principle.

As a matter of fact, it's a bit like when you drop your $1000 smartphone face against the ground: it is both broken and intact until you check its status!

The principle of superposition is the consequence of another principle in fundamental physics: the **wave-particle duality**.

We have all learned Physics, less or more, at high school, college or university. Remember the glorious photons, these grains of light that surround us, these kinds of tiny energy balls that hit our body without being felt.

Isaac Newton, the famous physicist of the eighteenth century, to whom we owe the foundations of Classical Mechanics (not that of cars, but that of planets, falling apples, etc.), believed that light was a flood of materials, of particles. He contradicted another physicist, Huygens, who thought that light was a wave.

It was not until the early nineteenth century that Thomas Young proves that light is a wave, like the pretty wavelets left by the pebble that is thrown into the water.

But who was right? Newton or Huygens/Young?

Einstein and Max Planck won the deal in 1905, by demonstrating one of the key concepts of Quantum Physics: wave-particle duality.

The photon is therefore both a wave and a particle.

You can visualize this concept by remembering these trendy baby toys in wood or plastic where the children have to slip shapes in the cutouts of a box. The photon is a kind of wooden cylinder. Depending on the direction, the cylinder may slip into a circle-shaped cutout or a rectangle-shaped cutout.

This principle of superposition also exists in Classical Mechanics: if you play two strings simultaneously on a guitar, you can consider that the air around the two strings "vibrates" in superposition on these two notes that are waves. However, there is a big difference with Quantum Physics: if you play a chord on the 6 strings of a guitar, you get an overlay of 6 states (or notes). In the quantum world, you would have obtained the equivalence of 2^6 states, or 128 states.

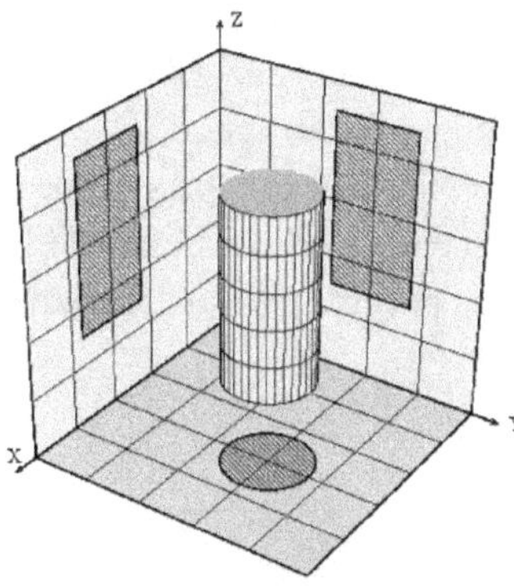

Figure 2: Photon duality

The principles of Quantum Mechanics were laid down at the beginning of the 20th century by two great scientists, Paul Dirac [2] and John von Neumann [3]. Today, these principles remain almost unchanged. They are so insensitive and surprising that even Einstein had doubts about some aspects of Quantum Physics. It is a French physicist, Alain Aspect, who confirmed these principles in the 60s.

By the way, Quantum Physics is not foreign to all of us. The transistor, the integrated circuit (IC) and the laser are based on these principles that built the first computer revolution of the twentieth century. It is their mathematical, physical and technological understanding that is leading us to this new level of technological evolution, Quantum Computing.

The quantum states can match to the **polarization** of a photon or to the **spin** of an electron. At the atomic and subatomic level, it's a bit more complex (and weird).

Spin is an intrinsic quantum property of a particle related to its angular or kinetic moment, that is to say the state of rotation of the particle. This property is as important as the mass or the electric charge of the particle. It has no equivalent in Classical Physics.

We can try to imagine this quantum kinetic moment as if the particle had a shape of ball that would turn on itself with respect to the axis of the direction of its propagation. This is only an image because the reality is much more complex. In particular, if the example of the ball was true, some elements of the ball should spin at a speed higher than that of light, which is impossible, as you know.

The photon has no mass. It's very easy to understand the notion of polarization as a kind of circular orientation to the right (clockwise) or left (counterclockwise), as if the photon was propagating in the form of a propeller. Its spin is equal to 1. Just for the fun of knowledge, may I mention that the photon is a tough particle whose life span is 10^{18} years.

Unlike the photon, the electron, which is a fermion, has a non-null mass and a spin of ½.

SUMMARY

- ✓ THE PRINCIPLE OF SUPERPOSITION IS A KEY CONCEPT OF QUANTUM COMPUTING.

- ✓ QUANTUM COMPUTING IS BASED ON STATISTICAL PRINCIPLES, THAT IS, ON THE PROBABILITY THAT A PARTICLE IS IN SPECIFIC STATE.

- ✓ QUANTUM PHYSICS IS DEEPLY DIFFERENT FROM CLASSICAL PHYSICS WE KNOW AND HAVE BEEN TAUGHT IN COLLEGE.

2.   WHAT IS A « QUBIT »?

The qubit is the quantum equivalence of the bit, our old binary pal of classical computers.

Without diving too far into Mathematics, you can imagine a qubit as a transparent plastic sphere with an arrow attached to the center of the sphere, of length equal to the radius of the sphere and which can point to any point of the surface of the sphere.

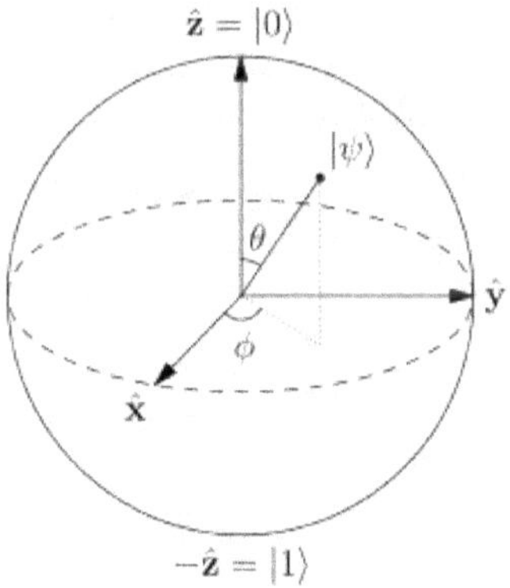

Figure 3: Bloch Sphere

This is the Bloch Sphere, a practical representation of qubit and its state.

In case of an elementary and classical logical information unit (the famous bits 0 or 1), consider that the arrow can only point upwards ("1") or downwards ("0"). So we have two states only.

In case of a qubit, the arrow is completely free to point to any point on the sphere surface. So we get an infinite number of states. For the mathematical skilled readers, please note that a qubit, at least its state, can be represented by a complex vector of norm equal to 1. If 2 qubits are grouped, their state is described by a 2x2 matrix, with 4 coefficients of complex numbers.

SUPERPOSITION

We know that a classical bit can only represent the logical values 0 or 1. As we have discovered in Schrödinger's cat history, the qubit can take both values simultaneously. It must be understood that it is not a question of uncertainty on the value 0 or 1 but of the superposition of two states 0 and 1 simultaneously. Imagine that you flip a coin which fell on both sides at the same time.

This may seem weird or impossible, but it is nevertheless the quantum reality proven by both Mathematics and experimentation.

May I recommend to the reader who has some notions of Mathematics and Linear Algebra to refer to the last chapter of this book to get the amazing mathematical explanation.

QUBIT : ANALOG OR DIGITAL OBJECT?

In this book, we will often talk about a qubit as a two-level quantum system or states that match to the discrete states of the classical bits, 0 and 1. In reality, though a qubit has discrete levels, there is actually an infinite number of possible states for one qubit, not just two. The qubit is therefore a kind of hybrid being, both logical and analog…

You can also imagine that an electron can be in two places at once. This notion is difficult to understand but the world of electrons is a very special one. It's also called superposition.

If you consider a molecule of O_2, aka oxygen, the two oxygen atoms actually share two pairs of electrons (the famous double covalent bond). Electrons are not "in the middle" but *are* in *both* atoms at the *same* time! As a matter of fact, the two atoms hence "stick" together. If there were no superposition, our molecules would collapse into several atoms (and our bodies too!).

Even Einstein did not believe in the principle of superposition until his death.

ENTANGLEMENT

Entanglement is another key point of Quantum Computing. Two qubits can form a system with entanglement, which means that the state of the system can be known independently of the state of the qubits that compose it. It's a kind of **correlation** between the two qubits. If we observe one of the qubits, we can know what is the state of the other qubit if it is measured in the same way. Even if the other qubit is at the end the universe.

In case of entanglement, the state of a qubit, 0 or 1, may depend on the state of the other entangled qubit.

You can understand this phenomenon by considering that the system is in a known and defined state but that its components are not.

How to make qubits entangled? By getting them closer to one another and performing some special operations.

Once two qubits are entangled, it is possible to separate them arbitrarily from each other, even from several million kilometers. Even so, they will remain entangled.

The entangled qubits are monogamous! Once entangled together, nothing can share this state of entanglement with them.

Experts sometimes use the term **supercorrelation** because it's possible to change the global state of the entangled qubits by changing the state of only one qubit.

You may possibly read that entanglement is a kind of instantaneous action at distance, whatever the distance. This is false: there is no action or communication of information but only a correlation that can only be known after the measurement of the states.

" By the Force of entangled qubits, intrigued you will be ".

BELL GAMES

In the 60s, physicist John Stewart Bell designed atypical mind games to better understand the principle of entanglement. Imagine two players physically isolated from each other. We ask each one the same simple question. To win, they must answer in a coordinated way but they have no way of communicating together. Who's answering first is entirely random. Each one has to guess what the answer of the other might be. Bell proved that if both players were able to share a pair of entangled particles, they would increase the correlation of their answers and thus their expectation of gain.

For the most curious readers, I cannot help but talk to you about Holevo's Theorem, also called *Holevo's Limit*. This theorem reminds us that nothing is obvious in Quantum Computing. Consider a system composed of n qubits. Thanks to the superposition principle, this system can have several simultaneous states, 2^n. However Holevo demonstrated that one could access at best at only n bits of information. Surprising, isn't it?

LOGICAL QUBIT & PHYSICAL QUBIT

I stated that cloning qubits is not possible. This constraint implies that it is not trivial to implement error control systems in Quantum Computing whereas this is relatively easy in Classical Computing.

An error control system can detect and/or fix errors. In conventional logic, you just have to add *control* bits that are mathematically related to the data bits they need to control. Depending on the number of control bits, it thus becomes possible to detect and/or fix one or more data bits.

Barcode EAN-13 coding system is a well-known example. The last digit of the code can detect any error in the first 12 digits. However, there is no error correction, only detection.

One of the great advances of Quantum Computing has been the development of quantum algorithms for error detection and correction and then the embedding of these error processes at the quantum circuit level.

It's why experts use the wording **logical qubit** which is a *good* qubit built by several physical qubits in charge of computation and error control.

In 2015, Google proposed an innovative quantum processor architecture designed to self-correct. With five and then nine qubits, the system was able to handle its own memory errors.

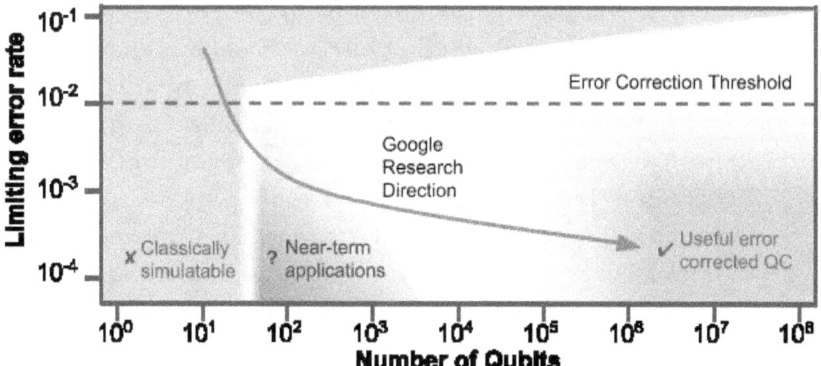

Figure 4: Relationship between number of qubits and error rate (Google Labs)

MEASURE & COHERENCE

Measuring a qubit does not really mean taking a multimeter to check the voltage of its wall outlet. The measure of a qubit is more like a question you ask to the qubit: *"dear qubit, are you looking up or down?"*. Our qubits are so shy that the mere fact of asking this question disturbs their state.

Even if a qubit may be in a superposition state, the process to measure it (measurement), will always result in one of its two states corresponding to 0 or 1 (under the metaphor of the classical computer logic). That means that every time you measure the qubit, it loses irreversibly any specific quantum character. That has important consequences on how to work with qubits.

So how to measure the state of a qubit? I'll use a graphical analogy to try to explain how this is possible. By the way please keep in mind that in reality, there are several types of technical devices to do it.

UNAUTHORIZED COPY

Every day, you use the famous copy/paste command. You don't worry too much whether our good old bits that code our data are copiable or not. In the quantum world you should because it is not possible to copy or even to clone qubits. The mathematical proof goes far beyond the scope of this book. Just be aware that it is only possible to copy some qubits that are in particular states. This non-cloning theorem has very important (and binding) implications for the programming of quantum computers in terms of information storage as well as propagation of the intermediate results of computations.

Consider a qubit with 4 states among all the possible states (remember the arrow that points inside the Bloch Sphere).

The "0" is symbolized by the orange up-arrow and the "1" by the yellow down-arrow (Z axis). We already know these two states; let's add the states that correspond to the X axis of the Bloch Sphere. Call them "+" and "-", symbolized by orange arrows to the left and to the right, respectively.

Now imagine two measuring devices.

With some basic Mathematics, let's say that one of the devices measures on the X axis, the second on the Z axis, which can be represented as a slot that allows (or not) the qubit to pass thru. (we simplify this point excessively but voluntarily). The measure gives either -1 or +1.

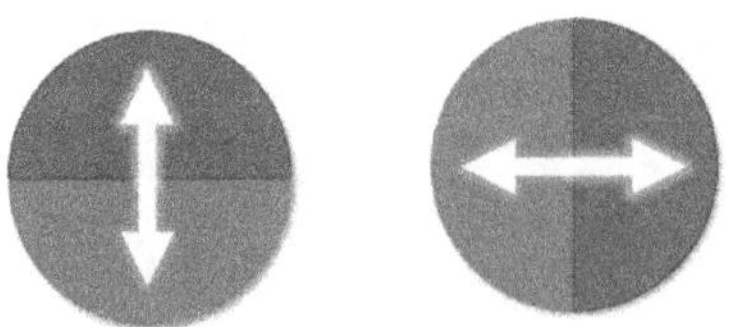

As we are in the Quantum World, we know that nothing normally happens, at least in the normality we are used to. Our measuring devices therefore have some special characteristics :

- If we measure on the X-axis, here are the possible results:

    o   If the qubit is in the state "0", 100% of probability of result equals to +1, the state of the qubit does not change, so we know its state.

    o   If the qubit is in the state "-", 50% of probability of result equals to -1, 50% of probability of result equals to +1, the state of the qubit changes.

    o   Etc.

- If we measure on the Z-axis, here are the possible results:

    o   If the qubit is in the state "-", 100% of probability of result equals to +1, the state of the qubit does not change, so we know its state.

    o   If the qubit is in the state "0", 50% of probability of result equals to +1, 50% of probability of result equals to -1, the state of the qubit changes.

    o   Etc.

We therefore conclude that it is mandatory to choose a measurement axis of a qubit and that any measurement modifies the quantum state of the qubit. That's not going to make easy the life of the designers of quantum computers!

HOW TO BUILD QUBITS ?

Making qubits is a daunting task, even in the lab. Getting good qubits, which are not very sensitive to ambient noise and with a high coherence time is even more complex.

It must be understood that researchers must work at extremely low energy levels, which means, whatever the technology used, that the system must evolve at very low temperatures.

When I say very low temperatures, I don't mean those of your freezer (around -18 ° C) but temperatures close to absolute zero, that is to say close to -273 ° C (or 0 Kelvin, unit commonly used in Physics). In short, it's cold, it's even very cold (the cold of the interstellar vacuum) and it requires specific high-performance cryogenic cooling systems.

There are currently 5 main types of technologies for creating qubits:

- Superconductor

- NV-Center

- Trapped-Ion

- Spin

- Topological

Each of the technologies has its advantages and its drawbacks.

For example, Intel works on several qubit technologies, including spin technology based on classical silicon processes, which are well mastered for decades.

SUPERCONDUCTOR QUBIT

In 1991, Heike Kammerlingh discovered that the electrical resistance of metals can become null (zero) at very low temperatures. This phenomenon surprised the entire scientific community, which expected a linear decline in resistance and not a sudden drop as experienced. The explanation of this quantum phenomenon, *superconductivity*, took more than fifty years. It is due to a special pairing of two electrons at very low temperature, known as Cooper Pair.

There are many types of superconductors qubits: by electric charge, by magnetic flux, by phase, fluxonium type, transmon type (a subtype of electrically charged qubits, etc.).

Most of these qubits are manufactured on regular standard chips (dies). Despite their short life, they have an interesting coherence time. This technique also makes the manipulation of the qubit states relatively easy with electromagnetic pulses. That makes it possible to design universal logic functions but also to easily couple the qubits between them.

On the other hand, superconductivity requires working in 200-liter containers with complex cryogenic systems that consume a lot of energy.

JOSEPHSON JUNCTIONS

Modern Electronics had been built using semiconductor technology that replaced the good old tubes or valves of the antic radios of our great grandparents. This technology is based on a junction between two differently doped semiconductors which can behave as a kind of controllable switch.

A similar effect can exist between two superconductors separated by a layer of insulator or metal: that is the Josephson effect. This effect is used in Josephson Junctions to create qubits. It is a very promising technology in terms of achievable operating frequency but which remains difficult to control because of the noise level.

NV CENTER QUBIT

One can also create qubits thanks to particular defects inside diamond crystal structure, called *nitrogen-vacancy center*, or **NV Center**. The identification of these defects is facilitated by its photoluminescence property: red light emission in the visible range during excitation with a specific wavelength laser.

A nitrogen atom has substituted in the crystal structure next to a missing carbon atom, hence the term *vacancy*. In this vacancy, electrons may be trapped and their spin can be used to form a qubit.

This innovative technology has several advantages: very long coherence time (around a second!) and wide range operation temperatures including ambient temperature.

Another nice advantage is that the spin of the electron is not the only qubit of the system: it may be coupled to the spin of the nuclei of the surrounding atoms that can serve as a kind of quantum storage space. It can also interact with photons which facilitates entanglement.

Current experiments are typically at 4K (-269.15°C) which is almost a "torrid" temperature compared to those requested by other technologies. The spin may be controlled via microwave pulses. The measurement is achieved by laser and detection of a possible emitted photon regarding the spin.

In 2018, researchers of the University of Delft managed to cope with the issues related to structural defects (presence of 1% of Carbon 13 with a spin of ½, which is troublesome). They were able to demonstrate the possibility of creating a quantum gate and succeeded to create a 1.3 km entanglement between two quantum systems based on NV center qubits.

TRAPPED-ION QUBITS

Photons may be entangled with a parent atom that contains some kinds of cavity. The energy levels of each ion represent the '0' and '1' states of the corresponding qubit. This technique uses electromagnetic pulses or lasers to excite the transition between the two energy levels. That thus simulates logic gates.

Researchers use different types of ions according to the requested features: for example, Calcium ions can store quantum information and Strontium ions can transfer this information.

The IonQ company specialized in this technology and in December 2018 announced a system of more than 11 qubits fully connected and 55 pairs of addressable qubits with a very good error rate: <1.0% on a gate to two qubits. Qubits are based on Ytterbium atoms, a rare element. They are trapped in a silicon support thanks to magnetic fields. The connection between the qubits is done by laser and entanglement.

SPIN QUBITS

This technology uses the spin of electrons that are controlled by microwave pulses. It is possible to place electrons in a state of superposition where they have at the same time a spin of "1" and a spin of "0".

The spin qubits has some advantages against their superconductor cousins:

- They are smaller and with less loss of coherence, which is a major advantage with quantum systems of several thousand or even millions of qubits.

- Their manufacturing process is close to the traditional well-known silicon-based process.

- They operate at cooler temperatures. It is very relative, but we talk about 1K (Kelvin, temperature unit, equal to -273.15°C, absolute zero) instead of 20 mK (millikelvin, one thousandth of Kelvin) for superconductors. This temperature difference is notable in terms of complexity, technical constraints, system dimensions, energy needs and overall cost.

- The design and production technology makes it possible to consider integrating high-performance communication systems directly at the level of qubits and silicon (multiplexed communication bus) and to limit the interconnections between qubits.

TOPOLOGICAL QUBITS

These qubits are based on exotic particles called anions. Although quite complex to implement, they have the advantage of being natively powerful tools for error correction.

Research is still in its infancy in this domain.

SUMMARY

- ✓ A QUBIT IN SUPERPOSITION MAY HAVE AN INFINITY OF STATES.

- ✓ ENTANGLEMENT BINDS TWO QUBITS TOGETHER.

- ✓ ENTANGLEMENT AND SUPERPOSITION ARE THE KEY PRINCIPLES OF QUANTUM COMPUTING.

- ✓ ANY MEASURE OF A QUBIT STATE DESTROYS THE QUANTUM STATE OF THE QUBIT.

- ✓ IT'S IMPOSSIBLE TO COPYCAT A QUBIT.

- ✓ A LOGICAL QUBIT IS A SYSTEM OF SEVERAL PHYSICAL QUBITS

3.   TELEPORTATION, MR. SPOCK

Teleportation has always been one of the biggest fantasies about Quantum Physics.

I'm really sorry to disappoint some of my readers, but the notion of quantum teleportation has little to do with the teleportation you know in sci-fi ghostbusters. There is only one similarity: the *original* is destroyed once teleported.

When we deal with quantum teleportation, we are talking about the transmission of a quantum state by sharing an entanglement (photon or electron) between the transmitter and the receiver. The famous researchers Bennett and Brassard introduced this concept in 1993 [4].

Precisely, quantum teleportation consists in transmitting the quantum state of an atom, an electron or a photon, from one place to another, after exchange of an entanglement between these two places and using a classic communication path. So it is information that is "*teleported*" and not matter. We are talking about communication and not about transportation.

No qubit is really moving. Each qubit is associated with 2 conventional bits that will pass through the conventional communication channel. May I add to your disappointment: that means that this transmission of information cannot be carried out at a speed greater than that of light since the reconstruction of the quantum information requires the transport of the conventional bits.

In the current state of research, we only know how to transfer the information associated with a few qubits between two entangled atoms. We are therefore still very far from teleporting the quantum state of complex molecules.

TELEPORTATION : ARE YOU SERIOUS?

Scientists are currently unable to teleport a human being or even a simple and basic object. However, the concept of teleportation would not violate any fundamental law of physics, nor even the famous principle of uncertainty which forbids the extraction of all information from a single atom not to say from an object. The skeptical reader might point out that if it is impossible to extract enough information from an object to be able to make a faithful copy, it would not be possible to teleport it.

Nope! There is a new paradox in Quantum Physics known as the Einstein-Podolsky-Rosen effect. To make it simple, let's say that one just needs to use an intermediate object that would be entangled with the copied object (but not with the one to be copied!).

There are commercial devices that can establish a quantum connection typically over dozens of km, with a maximum of 200 km. However, Chinese researchers have achieved the feat (in the state of current technologies in 2019) to achieve a quantum teleportation over 1400 km between the Earth and a satellite in orbit.

It's also possible to swap the entanglement.

Researchers are currently considering creating a Quantum Internet at the worldwide level, which would allow secure exchange of encryption keys, time synchronization, anonymization, and complex problem solving in distributed environments (that means multiple computers connected together to perform the same calculation in a shared and optimized way).

Communication can be achieved by optical fiber, point-to-point optical over-the-air link or satellite link.

The advantage of optical fiber is that this network already exists and is used by all the telecommunications companies of the world. Since the attenuation of an optical fiber is an exponential function of distance, it is not possible to exceed a few dozens of kilometers without using **quantum repeaters**. Unfortunately, these repeaters are much more complex than simple amplifiers or re-injectors of optical signals. Remember that quantum information cannot be amplified or copied!

SUMMARY

- ✓ ONLY INFORMATION CAN BE TELEPORTED, NOT OBJECTS.

- ✓ THE PRINCIPLE OF QUANTUM TELEPORTATION DOES NOT INFRINGE ANY LAW OF GENERAL PHYSICS OR QUANTUM PHYSICS.

- ✓ THE QUANTUM TRANSMISSION OF INFORMATION IS DONE AT A SPEED LESS THAN THAT OF LIGHT.

4. WHAT IS A QUANTUM COMPUTER?

A quantum computer is a very complex system which can manipulate and control qubits just as a conventional computer does with traditional bits. We will discover that, in the Quantum World, the adjective "*complex*" really matters!

I'd like to quote Bo Ewlad, CEO of the start-up ColdQuanta, "*a quantum computer does not know how to make an addition, not even a subtraction, in fact it does not know how to do much of what we usually expect from a computer*".

Nowadays, a quantum computer is basically a kind of computational (quantum) accelerator coupled to a conventional computer. The concept is similar to the accelerator graphics card that you can buy to increase the performance of your PC for video games or, more professionally, the accelerator card to optimize calculations in Artificial Intelligence.

To build a quantum computer, you need to assembly several components:

- A quantum chip, with qubits inside, whatever the qubit technology you have selected;

- A control-and-command subsystem which manages control signals for qubits. It depends on the qubit technology you have selected;

- A quantum (analog) computing to classical (digital) computing conversion subsystem;

- A data exchange and transmission architecture (some kind of communication bus) between all the components and the control signals;

- A microarchitecture for translating the instructions set to control signals;

- An instructions set;

- A computational unit dedicated to arithmetical (classical or quantum) computations;

- A programming language and its compiler;

- Specific quantum algorithms;

- Command and control software and hardware;

- Error detection and correction software and hardware.

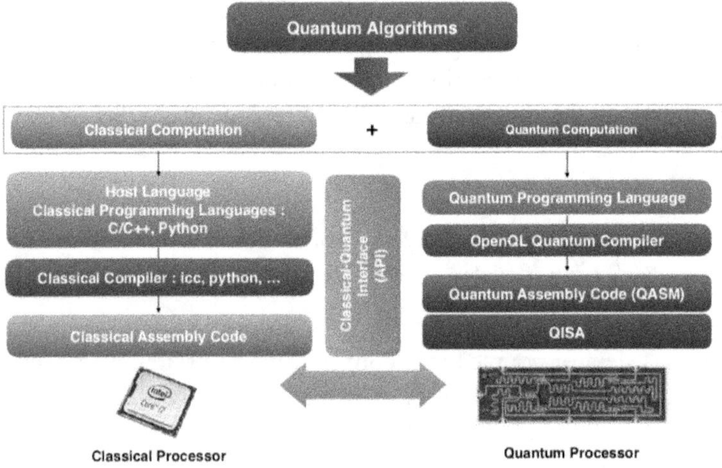

Figure 5: Architecture of a Quantum Computer (Delft University)

QUANTUM CHIP

At the heart of a traditional computer, there is the microprocessor whose leading manufacturers are Intel, AMD, Freescale or Qualcomm. These microprocessors contain billions of transistors which process bits, these basic chunks of data.

Similarly, the quantum chip is at the heart of the quantum computer.

This is the quantum chip that will host the qubits whatever the technology and materials used. The quality and manufacturing accuracy of these materials must be extreme in terms of uniformity, chemical composition, crystallographic structure and electrical properties.

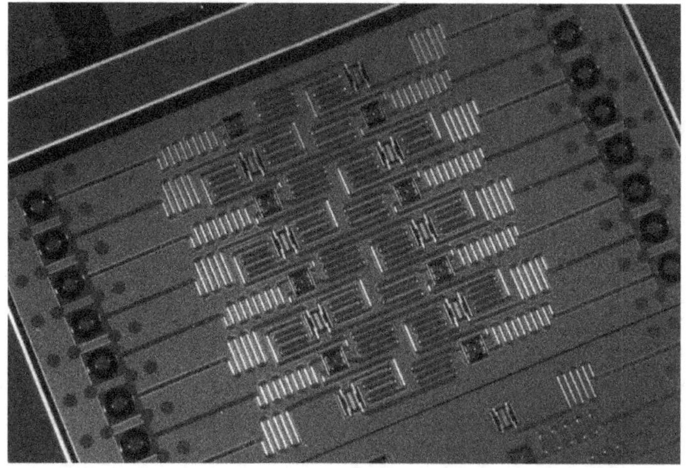

Figure 6: 16-qubit Processor of IBM

In 2018, the Google Quantum AI Lab announced its first quantum processor of 72 qubits, based on its 9-qubit technology. With error rates in reading of 1%, in logical 1-qubit quantum function of 0.1% and in logical 2-qubit quantum function of 0.6%, it was very promising. These logical functions are called *gates*. We will discuss further about that concept.

Figure 7: 72-qubit Processor of Google

The semiconductor industry has well-honed manufacturing processes in terms of accuracy, even for mass production.

Moreover, the most interesting qubit technologies at present are whose manufacturing processes are closest to those of semiconductors.

A first dilemma arises: by construction, the qubits are often isolated and yet they will have to communicate while preserving a maximum coherence time, which is often contradictory.

Quantum Computing is based on the two very particular properties of qubits: superposition and entanglement. Thanks to these two principles, it is possible to use qubits as very sophisticated types of switches. As a matter of fact, modern computers are based on switches and all the computer logic that we know today can be expressed mathematically by a combination of switches (gates).

Qubits manipulation depends on the technology used to create the qubits. For example, if ions and their excitation states are worked on, the manipulations are performed with laser beams, by varying the excitation time or the wavelength of the laser. If, on the other hand, particles with spin are used, the manipulations are done by applying magnetic fields of several orientations.

Since a quantum state has a limited lifetime (coherence time), it is necessary to ensure excellent synchronization and a perfect time base of all the control signals.

DiVincenzo Criteria

In 2000, the physicist David DiVincenzo enunciated [5] the five mandatory and fundamental criteria, since called DiVicenzo Criteria, to build a quantum computer, as well as two criteria for quantum communication.

This five criteria are:

- Qubits must be clearly defined in terms of quantum state. We must be able to add some qubits to the system if needed. The system must remain scalable.

- It is necessary to be able to initialize the qubits in a known quantum state. The time required to initialize the qubits must be less than their coherence time, which is not always easy technologically speaking.

- It is necessary to have a set of universal quantum gates which makes it possible to model all the computations.

- It should be possible to measure specific qubits. It is sometimes necessary to carry out several measurements (and thus to carry out the same calculation several times) in order to obtain the statistically most probable result.

- The coherence time must be long enough to allow calculations to terminate. Specific states of superposition and entanglement must be preserved as long as possible.

QUBITS LOVE THE COLD

Most technologies for designing qubits require extremely low operating temperatures, very close to absolute zero.

It has therefore been necessary to develop specific cooling systems. But qubits are very sensitive to vibrations and magnetic or electric noises, not to mention temperature variations that have a direct impact on energy levels.

The solution currently used in Quantum Computing is based on the cryogenic technology called **dilution refrigerator** invented by Heinz London in 50s in laboratory and then, in collaboration with Oxford Instruments, carried out in practice in 1967 with a temperature of 200 mK (-272.95°C). The process consists of mixing two helium isotopes in liquid phases (3He and 4He, which are respectively a fermion and a boson, but you already knew it!).

Today, 4 mK can easily been achieved thanks to this technology. For comparison, the space is much warmer, at 2.7 K!

To perform computations on qubits, there are kinds of gates, also called *quantum operators* (*quantum gates*), which make it possible to build a quantum logic, just as conventional computers are built around a binary logic.

There are currently two main major paradigms in Quantum Computing:

- QA - Quantum Annealing Model, whose promoters are D-Wave Systems, Google and NASA. This architecture is quite particular and limited in terms of quantum algorithms. However, systems of this type already have several thousand qubits.

- QM - Gate Model, which is more general and independent of a particular manufacturer. IBM and Rigetti Computing are the promoters of this architecture. They offer tools and access to their quantum computers via the Cloud. In 2019, these systems do not exceed a few dozens of qubits.

QUANTUM ANNEALING MODEL

The Quantum Annealing Model refers to the *annealing* term that comes from metallurgy (alternation of cooling and reheating to minimize the energy of a material). Indeed, a material does not always cool in a structure that is ideal (at minimum energy state). There may be several minimum states called *candidates*. Only the annealing method makes it possible to "browse" the different candidates and to find the one that is really the minimum energy state.

At the quantum level, this notion corresponds to a mode of computation which makes it possible to find the minimum of a given function among a finite set of possible solutions thanks to quantum fluctuations. Possible solutions are represented by possible quantum states that are superposed with equal (probabilistic) weights. The quantum system is then allowed to evolve over time to a state of minimal energy.

Programming this type of quantum computer involves to formalize a problem of finding the minimum solution corresponding to the best possible result. The quantum processor will then consider all possible solutions simultaneously and return the minimal energy solutions. Among this set of solutions (the energy minima) is the best solution.

Figure 8: Quantum Chip of D-Wave Systems with 128 quantum items

In 2007, D-Wave Systems, a Canadian company, officially announced a quantum computer based on 16 qubits.

Several experts (and competitors) criticized and questioned the technical and technological choices of the company: "*All qubits are not equal*", arguing that the D-Wave system was not really a quantum computer. In particular, it cannot execute the famous Shor's Algorithm which makes it possible to factorize an integer into a polynomial at a non-exponential time.

Despite the voices of its detractors, the D-Wave solutions were of interest to Google, which launched in 2013 the Quantum Artificial Intelligence Lab, hosted by NASA's Ames Research Center. Google has since experimented with a 512-qubit D-Wave quantum computer. D-Wave qubits are based on superconducting Josephson Junction technology.

As you have probably understood, the D-Wave technology is particularly suited to optimization problems, like search of the best combination of certain elements while respecting a set of constraints. For example: optimizing radiation intensity in cancer radiotherapy, optimizing car traffic, improving marketing strategies for recruiting new clients.

By the way, D-Wave's teams have been able to implement a hybrid architecture that effectively resolves other classes of problems such as political forecasting and polls or facial recognition in Machine Learning (one of the branches of Artificial Intelligence).

In 2019, D-Wave has delivered the 2,000 qubit D-Wave 2000Q for sale or for real-time cloud access and several open-source development tools.

QUANTUM GATE MODEL

The Quantum Gate model is the physical model the closest to the Classical Computing model that uses logical functions (gates): quantum gates, quantum I/O ports and quantum interconnections between gates and I/O ports. That looks definitely like a good old integrated circuit.

Programming can be very similar to classical programming with the help of an abstraction layer. It's a key winning point.

It has been demonstrated in Classical Computing that any computation can be broken down into a set of elementary logical gates of a single type. So-called **quantum gates** have a behavior very similar to conventional logic gates. They have inputs and outputs and can be combined to create more sophisticated functions.

Thus, unlike Quantum Annealing computers, Quantum Gate computers are universal. It is obviously necessary to write low-level specific modules but the current trend is to standardize interfaces and quantum programming languages.

The competition is already tough in Quantum Computing: IBM offers a kind of annealing emulation like D-Wave Systems using a logic gate model! The converse is not true because a quantum annealing system cannot simulate a quantum gate model (at least in a polynomial and non-exponential execution time).

HYBRID ARCHITECTURE

The near future of the quantum computer is probably in a kind of hybridization with a classical computer where the quantum part plays the role of specialized accelerator, much like a graphics card on a computer intended for video games.

Just like with a graphics accelerator card, the main program runs on the classic computer, with bytes of code natively intended to the quantum computer.

Most quantum computer architecture design research is currently done in this spirit, either directly at the chip level (hybridization on silicon), or with a very high speed communication bus. Do not forget computers and systems that control the entire environment necessary for the quantum computer (cryogenics, etc.) and those that manage command and control electromagnetic signals or lasers.

QUANTUM AND PARALLELISM

We often read in articles or books that quantum computing is parallelism. It's wrong. A quantum computer of n qubits is not equivalent to 2^n computers that would work in parallel. It is less powerful, especially because it is not deterministic.

A quantum computer will not be faster than a conventional computer for an elementary operation. This is even the opposite because the "useful" operating frequency of a quantum computer is not very high because of intrinsic constraints. What is innovative is its ability to strongly optimize some types of calculations using specific algorithms that cannot run on a conventional computer.

I'd like to provide a relatively simple analogy to make you feel the extreme complexity of the architecture of a quantum computer. Consider our good old Internet. Everyone knows that you can send and receive data packets from your computer to another computer without worrying too much about the place, the brand, the operating system and the software.

When I order a book on Amazon, I do not care if the ecommerce server is located in a datacenter in Frankfurt or in Seattle. I'm not even supposed to know that Amazon has developed its own operating system. This simplicity is due, among other things, to the standardization of Internet protocols, particularly at the directory level (DNS - which guarantees to know *"who is who?"*) and to routing protocols that can be used to route data packets to their correct destination. If I take again the example of the Amazon website, I can type `www.amazon.com` in my browser, without worrying to consult the Yellow Pages of the Internet, ie the DNS server that gives me the physical-logical address (IP) of the Amazon server. I do not care either about the router at my ISP that will link to other routers from other providers, up to Amazon's server(s). Everything is done transparently for me and without any delay.

In Quantum Computing, developers will need an equivalent system to know where the qubits are at a given moment and what are the connections between them. It's like a qubits routing table. Even more complex, the system running the code (the program) on the qubit processor will have to adapt the instructions in real time according to the routing table and decide to perform qubit moves or optimize the instructions, if necessary to preserve the topology (locations) of the qubits.

It is easy to understand that moving a qubit requires actions at a very low level in the quantum machinery. Computer scientists and physicists must learn to talk to each other and understand how to optimize this complexity.

DEAR GOOFY QUBITS

Please keep in mind that qubits are currently extremely fragile beings with not very high duration of coherence and errors issues. It is therefore necessary to set up error correction systems, which are very resource-intensive (estimated in 2019 at 90% of the time spent by the quantum processor).

The complex calculations intended for quantum computers require a much lower error rate than what is currently achieved at the hardware level of these computers. Qubits should be protected of any external noise (thermal, signals, currents, magnetism, etc.) and controlled in the most precise possible way.

In the current state (2019) of quantum technologies, we do not know how to guarantee an intrinsic error of less than 1% whereas it would be necessary to reach 10^{-15} to carry out really useful calculations. Although important progress has been made in recent years, the only solution is to work in redundancy, by building a **logical qubit** from several physical qubits.

But unfortunately, measuring a qubit to find out if there is an error irreparably causes the loss of any superposition state. It is therefore necessary to be able to measure this potential error indirectly.

Auxiliary qubits (*ancilla*) which are coupled to the physical qubits are used for this purpose. They constitute what is called the logical qubit. These are the auxiliary qubits that will be measured to check if there is a problem.

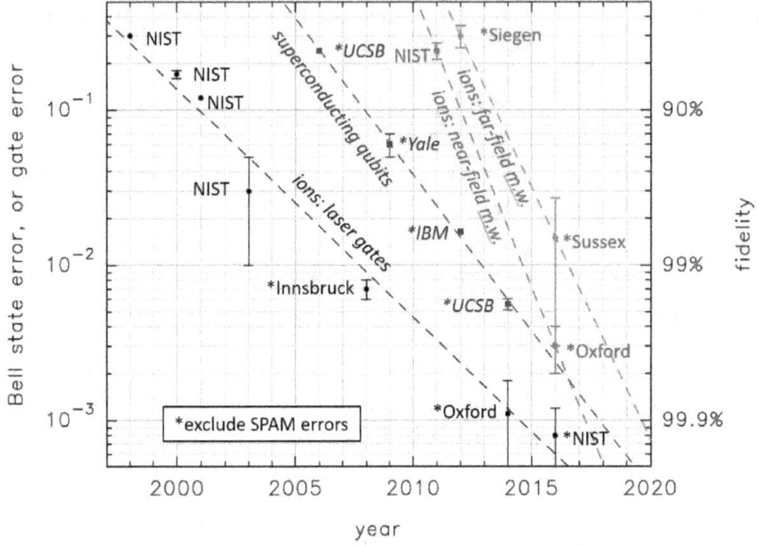

Figure 9: Accuracy evolution of 2-qubit quantum gate

The more physical (and auxiliary) qubits are added, the more effective the detection and correction of errors is. To achieve an error of 10^{-15}, it would need 10,000 qubits, which is far beyond current technological capabilities.

ENERGY SAVING

Energy optimization is an often overlooked feature of quantum computer which might consume far less than equivalent conventional computers, even with the constraints of cryogenics. Experts agree on 100 to 1000 times less power consumption, which is interesting in a world increasingly dominated by energy-burners like the Cloud and the IoT.

SUMMARY

✓ SEVERAL QUBITS TECHNOLOGIES ARE CURRENTLY ASSESSED, EACH WITH ITS ADVANTAGES AND ITS DRAWBACKS. FOR THE MOMENT, NO ONE IS PREDOMINANT.

✓ THE FOLLOWING METAPHOR CAN BE USED: THE QUANTUM ANNEALING MODEL IS QUASI ANALOG WHILE THE QUANTUM GATE MODEL IS QUASI DIGITAL.

✓ QUBITS INTERCONNEXION IS A REALLY BIG ISSUE AND RESTRICTS CURRENTLY DESIGN OF MORE ADVANCED ARCHITECTURE WITH MANY MORE QUBITS.

✓ 90% OF THE QUANTUM PROCESSOR TIME IS DEDICATED TO ERROR CORRECTION AT QUBIT LEVEL.

5.   THE QUANTUM INTERNET

First, let me quote Thomas Jennewein, well-known physicist of the Waterloo University: *"The term 'Quantum Internet' is vague. Many people, including me, like to use it. However, there is no real definition of its meaning"*.

Before building a Quantum Internet, researchers need to know how to build quantum networks, which interconnect several quantum computers capable of exchanging qubits.

We should also distinguish between small-distance quantum networks intended to distribute computations (*clusters* in Classical Computing) and those specialized in the exchange of data, generally over greater distances, because the constraints and the requested performances are quite different.

The Quantum Internet is equivalent to the Classical Internet except that quantum computers, instead of conventional computers, are connected to it. However, it is possible to design a quantum coupling interface for connecting conventional computers to the Quantum Internet.

The concept of this Quantum Internet is based on the two characteristics of entanglement: confidentiality and maximum coordination. Two qubits located at very long distances each other guarantee the secrecy of the transmissions since the state of entanglement cannot be shared and the reading (measurement) of the quantum state immediately drives to its collapse, which is easily detectable. The result of the measurement of this state is always the same regardless of the distance, which is very interesting to synchronize clocks.

As you know, nothing is simple in the Quantum World : these technologies have already been attacked exploiting some implementation vulnerabilities.

STATE OF THE ART

Since 2008, technology and research have advanced a lot in this area.

Between 2009 and 2011, CERN and the University of Geneva successfully developed and tested a quantum network, SwissQuantum. Their goal was to prove that it was possible to translate the researches of their respective laboratories into a production environment. The result had been a robust, reliable and interconnected network with existing conventional systems.

Under the leadership of the University of Delft in the Netherlands, researchers from the European Quantum Internet Alliance have been working since 2013 to set up an Internet consisting of end nodes (or terminal nodes), switches, repeaters and routers specific to Quantum Computing. The goal is to go beyond a quantum key distribution by allowing the interconnection of quantum processors with data sharing and distributed applications.

In 2014, a European team led by the University of Geneva managed the transfer of quantum information over 12 km from a quantum memory based on a doped crystal and via a traditional network of optical fibers. The difficulty was to have qubits (photons in this case) entangled at a frequency compatible with propagation in optical networks used by telecommunications operators. To make the task even more difficult, the wavelength usable by the quantum memory (883 nm) was different from that of the optical fiber (1338 nm).

In 2016, China launched the first quantum satellite to secure communications between multiple ground stations. This country plans to launch several other quantum satellites in the coming years.

In May 2019, the US Air Force Research Laboratory (AFLR) has achieved a quantum communication with a satellite link in daylight, which was impossible before. This technological step should allow quasi-permanent secure satellite communications.

BUSINESS CASES AND USAGES

What are the promises of the Quantum Internet and what applications are possible in the short or medium term?

Here are a few:

-   the main application is to establish secure communications via the quantum distribution of encryption keys;

- the second most important application is the synchronization of clocks and more generally of processes, for example with data distributed in the Cloud;

- more generally, to exploit distributed computing functionalities more efficiently than in conventional computing;

- to allow access to a central quantum computer in full security (confidentiality and integrity);

- to create clusters of small quantum computers that would be seen as larger quantum computers;

- to protect critical communication from malicious interference, eavesdropping or jamming.

WHY IS IT SO DIFFICULT TO TRANSMIT QUBITS OVER LONG DISTANCES?

To simplify your understanding, consider the hypothesis of a photon as a qubit. Just a photon, a small grain of light, which follows the famous laws of wave-particle duality. This photon is easy to lose in nature, even surrounded and protected by the inner walls of an optical fiber. It is therefore necessary to have quantum repeaters that use quantum teleportation, thanks to entanglement.

First you need to create two entangled qubits between the two network nodes. Imagine that the two network nodes are 200 km away. The laws of propagation of a photon in an optical fiber lead to an excessive loss of photons over this distance. You need to install a quantum repeater in the middle of the link, at 100 km, and to create the first two qubits entangled between the repeater and the first network node. This distance allows a transmission without too much loss. Then you replicate the process between the repeater and the second network node.

Note that the repeater must be protected against compromise and eavesdropping if you want to guarantee a fully secure communication.

A terminal node does not have to be a very complex quantum system. Currently, researchers evoke between 1 and 12 qubits, which corresponds to current technologies available. A single qubit can be enough to benefit from entanglement (which is only possible between two qubits).

It also requires switches to distribute traffic over optical fibers, some of which should have routing functions. These switches are more complex than current regular switches because they must maintain qubit consistency.

Finally, the architecture of this new Quantum Internet needs quantum repeaters in order to send qubits to the other end of the Earth. As it is not possible to copy the qubits, it is therefore not possible to use conventional optical repeaters.

As you already know, everything goes very fast in Quantum Computing: at the time of this book writing (May 2019), Chinese physicists have just demonstrated that it is possible for a classical computer to communicate privately and secured with a quantum computer. This means that you can delegate calculations to a quantum computer without the quantum computer having all the information about the calculation. We are talking about a *blind* mode. Until now only a quantum computer was able to do so with guaranteed confidentiality.

SUMMARY

- ✓ QUANTUM NETWORKS HAVE EXISTED FOR YEARS AND HAVE PROVIDED QUANTUM CIPHERING KEY DISTRIBUTION.

- ✓ SECURE HYBRID QUANTUM NETWORKS ACTUALLY EXIST USING FIBER OPTICS AND SATELLITE LINKS.

- ✓ DISTANCES ARE CURRENTLY LIMITED: 200 KM MAX (OPTIC FIBER).

- ✓ QUANTUM INTERNET DESIGN AND BUILD ARE COMPLEX (SPECIFIC SWITCHES, ROUTERS AND REPEATERS).

6.   QUANTUM ALGORITHMS

An *algorithm* is a sequence of elementary computations that solves a given problem or efficiently computes a result from a dataset.

Programming a quantum computer requires transforming a problem of the real world into a quantum language - or at least into an algorithm adapted to the quantum world - and solving the problem.

Quantum algorithms, however, have an important feature compared to the Classical Computing world. When you run a program (a sequence of algorithms) on your regular computer, you get *the* result. This result is unique and deterministic. If you run the program again, you get the *same* result (well, normally, but we're not immune to a bug...). On a quantum computer, you get *a* result. If you run the program again, chance is that you will get *another* result.

Quantum Computing is not deterministic but probabilistic.

So you need to execute several times a quantum algorithm on the same dataset and to keep only the most probable result. The sagacious reader will immediately have noticed that any reading of a qubit destroys its quantum state: so it's necessary to reset the input data at each new iteration of the same computation.

Quantum algorithms are classified according to the types (classes) of problems they solve. Here are some examples:

- The famous Shor's Algorithm which decomposes an integer into prime numbers. Since its speed is polynomial (relative to the size of the integer to be factored) on a quantum computer (whereas the speed of the corresponding algorithm is exponential on a classical computer), it allows, theoretically, to break systems of public key encryption such as the RSA or the Diffie-Hellman key exchange protocol which are based on the large integer factoring complexity. The result is the same for elliptic curve cryptography.

- The Grover's Algorithm which optimizes the graph processing and searches into databases.

- The Deutsch-Jozsa Algorithm which is a simple algorithm invented in 1985 and improved several times. It solves problems of the "decision with oracle" type. Behind this strange term lies the search for a solution that satisfies a value of a function. It was the first discovered quantum algorithm to be more efficient than its traditional counterpart.

- The Hallgren Algorithm which makes it possible to break certain types of cryptosystems in a polynomial time.

- Machine Learning Algorithms. A chapter of this book is devoted to the impacts of Quantum Computing on Artificial Intelligence.

- Markov chains or processes. A Markov chain is a series of random events where the future depends on the past only by the present. Some practical examples of Markov chains in everyday life: the number of people in a queue, the position of a car. There are many applications in many fields. Several quantum algorithms give better results than the classical Monte Carlo algorithm.

By the way, the domain of quantum algorithms evolves very quickly. This is a very exciting field of investigation for researchers and many start-ups are working on this topic, even before quantum computers have enough qubits for the algorithms they are designing.

In 2018, a young 18-year old student surprised everyone by demonstrating that conventional computers could solve a particular problem that only quantum computers were able to do quickly (exponentially), according to experts. This mathematical problem belongs to the same class of problems as well-known recommendation systems like those of Netflix or Amazon for example. He demonstrated that one of the most promising quantum algorithms (that of Kerenidis and Prakas) had no advantage over the classical algorithms, which put a chill on the quantum community!

SUMMARY

- ✓ QUANTUM COMPUTING IS NOT DETERMINISTIC BUT PROBABILISTIC. YOU HAVE TO KEEP IT IN MIND!

- ✓ FUTURE IS HYBRIDITY OF CLASSICAL AND QUANTUM ALGORITHMS.

- ✓ ARTIFICIAL INTELLIGENCE, ESPECIALLY MACHINE LEARNING IS A GOOD CANDIDATE FOR QUANTUM COMPUTING.

7.   WHAT IS A QUANTUM PROGRAM LIKE?

This is one of the questions I am most often asked in my seminars. How do you program a quantum computer? In assembler, in advanced language? With switches and lights like the very first computers? With thought?!

You have to understand that, for the moment, the use of a quantum computer, with a limited number of qubits, sounds more like using a graphic accelerator card (GPU) in a PC for video games.

It would be quite possible to run a complete game program onto a graphics card but it does not make sense in terms of efficiency, both in terms of technical code execution, algorithmic and coding. Thus, with a few exceptions, only the parts of the game program that deal with the graphics will be executed on the graphics card.

We find this type of architecture in a smartphone that usually integrates two processors: one for the telecommunications and radio parts, the other for other functions (operating system, human interface, apps).

It's the same paradigm for a quantum computer. Parts of the code will be executed on a conventional computer and other parts on the quantum computer.

Never forget that Quantum Computing is not deterministic but probabilistic. Remember that measuring the quantum state, that is, reading the result, means destroying the quantum superposition state.

Unlike classical computing, the same quantum algorithm will have to be run several times in order to obtain several results. *"The"* result is finally the one with the most occurrences, that is to say with the highest probability to be read.

The operation is therefore deeply different from classical computing. The designers must skillfully cut the code and distribute it between the two parts of the computer, classical or quantum. As with a graphical accelerator card, this distinction is made both manually by the programmer and automatically at the compiler level, this particular program that translates high-level languages such as C, Java or Python, in machine language, understandable by the computer and its microprocessor.

If we have a 4-qubit quantum computer, we can get a <u>simultaneous</u> superposition of 2^4 distinct logical states, which means 16 states. Yes, I did write *simultaneous*! If we are lucky enough to use a 32-qubit quantum computer, we get 2^{32} simultaneous logical states, which means more than 4 billion states!

As a comparison to the real world we know, imagine that I have 4 coins. If I am playing flip-flop with the four coins at the same time, I have 2^4 possibilities, but once the coins are thrown and dropped, I get only <u>one</u> 'result' among the 2^4 possibilities. Each result has a probability of $1/2^4$ (if the coins are ideal, not faked and no cheat). The 4 qubits of a quantum computer exist in 16 states <u>at the same time</u> which makes it possible to compute in a very effective way (it is however not parallelism).

QUANTUM DEVELOPMENT FRAMEWORKS

Most quantum computer vendors provide developers with a *framework*, which is a development environment that makes their work easier.

These vendors also offer access to their quantum machines, some for free but necessarily limited (like IBM) or for a fee for businesses. Access to these machines can be done via the Cloud.

As it can be seen in this example (screenshot of my IBM Quantum Cloud Services account), 4 machines are available, each with 2, 4, 5 and 16 qubits respectively. There are also simulators with several levels of complexity, and therefore usage costs.

IBM Q Backend Access

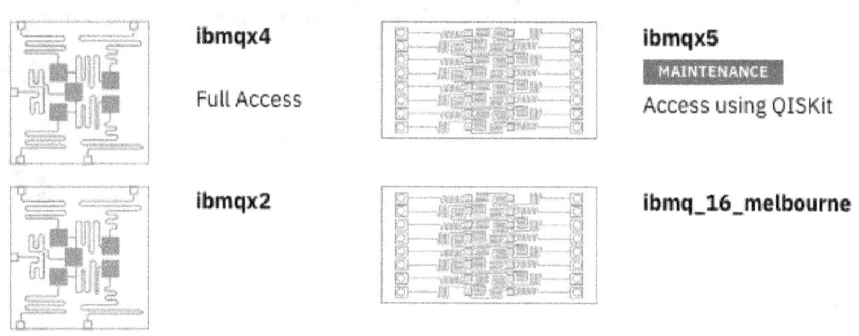

Figure 10: Example of Quantum Computers available on the Cloud (IBM)

Access to IBM quantum computers is done via a queue. It is possible to launch a query directly inside the code which gives the most available machine according to the number of qubits you want. You can then select dynamically during the execution of the code which quantum computer you want your program to use.

GRAPHICAL INTERFACE FOR QUANTUM PROGRAMMING

Quantum often means paradigm shift. There are several ways to program a quantum computer, from assembler (low-level language, also called machine language) to more advanced languages like Python, or layers of abstraction that almost completely hide quantum complexity from the programmer.

Quantum Gate Programming is one of the specials of Quantum Computing. It is interesting for researchers but also for programmers who want to understand or simulate the quantum limits of working at a level quite close to the material. You will find in the last chapter of this book a description of the main quantum gates commonly used.

IBM provides an online graphical programming interface that allows you to literally *draw* basic quantum programs, which could be called a *circuit*. The interface is called IBM Q Circuit Composer. It takes the standardized graphical elements of the quantum gates and allows to quickly create a circuit and generate the equivalent assembly code.

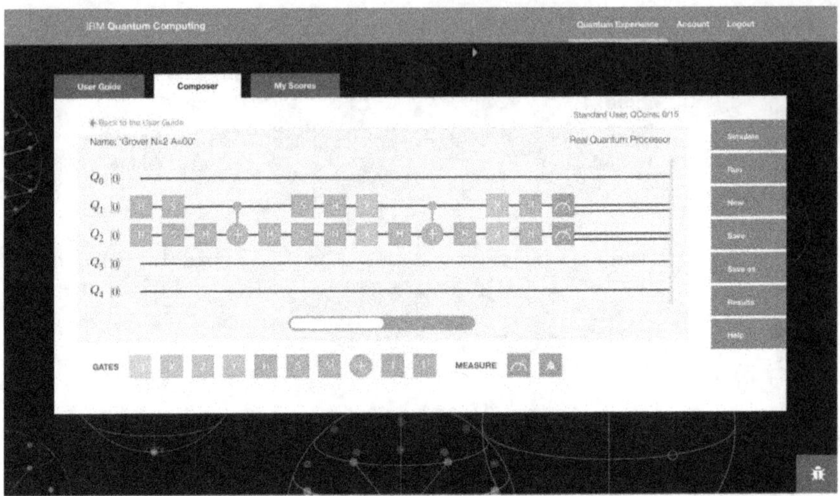

Figure 11: Graphical Quantum Programming Interface (IBM Q Circuit Composer)

YOUR FIRST QUANTUM PROGRAM

Now that you feel very powerful yourselves with access to real quantum computers, it's time to write a real quantum program!

Unhappily, time is now I cold some of my readers: you will not break an encryption algorithm or fold a complex protein. You are going to ... just flip coins.

I can hear you: "Damned! All this for a simple coin tossing game?" Yes ... but on a real quantum computer, anyway! More seriously, we face to two major difficulties. First, the knowledge needed to implement true quantum algorithms goes well beyond these few lines. Secondly, we are only going to work with 3 qubits, which limits our field of evaluation and investigation.

We will write this program in Python. Python is an interpreted (that is, non-compiled) programming language with a relatively simple syntax. It has become prevalent in many areas in recent years and is available on most current computing platforms. (Windows, MacOs, Linux, etc.).

If you do not know Python, do not worry: the syntax of the language makes it easy to understand "what's going on".

More advanced readers can install the IBM Qiskit framework and test the program themselves.

Go back to our coin tossing game. A coin is a two-state system: heads or tails. This is not unlike a qubit whose quantum state is a probabilistic distribution.

We will use this analogy to simulate the flip of 3 coins in the form of 3 qubits and a fairly simple quantum circuit that superposes the 3 qubits and allows to read the results.

For this small program, we need 3 qubits quantum registers, using `QuantumRegister`, and 3 classical "mirror" registers, using `ClassicalRegister`, so that we can read (measure) the result.

We'll use a very special quantum *gate*, the Hadamard gate, **H**, in order to place each of the 3 qubits in superposition state.

By default each qubit is initialized to a kind of '0' (for purists: $|0>$).

Thanks to the Qiskit framework, it's possible to visualize the circuit using `QuantumCircuit.draw`.

Code is below (on simulator first).

```
from qiskit import ClassicalRegister,
QuantumRegister, QuantumCircuit
from qiskit import execute
from qiskit import BasicAer
import numpy as np
backend =
BasicAer.get_backend('qasm_simulator')
q = QuantumRegister(3)
c = ClassicalRegister(3)
circuit = QuantumCircuit(q, c)
circuit.h(q[0])
circuit.h(q[1])
circuit.h(q[2])
circuit.measure(q, c)
print(QuantumCircuit.draw(circuit,
output='text'))
job = execute(circuit, backend, shots=100)
print(job.result().get_counts(circuit)
```

At runtime, we get the following result.

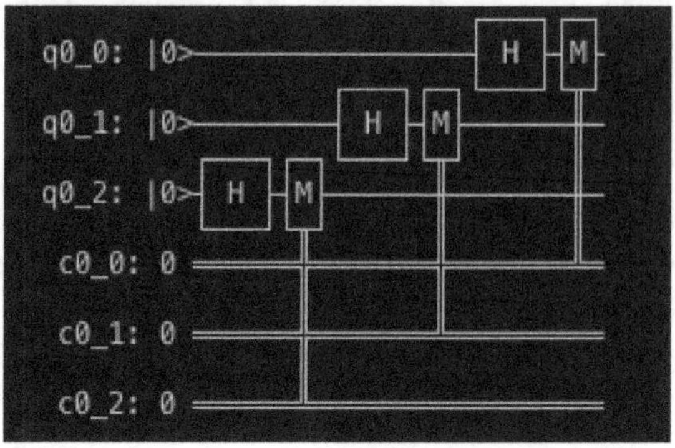

```
{'100': 15, '110': 10, '101': 9, '000':
14, '011': 16, '111': 12, '001': 12,
'010': 12}
```

Your result maybe different but it's quite normal. Here is an example of another runtime:

```
{'101': 9, '110': 16, '100': 14, '011':
10, '000': 17, '010': 15, '111': 11,
'001': 8}
```

We do have a probabilistic distribution on 100 flips of 3 coins. Mathematically, each combination should have the same probability but it would take, as in reality, well over 100 flips to get there.

Now we are going to run the program on a real quantum computer. As you can see, the code does not change much, except that we look in the Cloud for the least busy computer to perform our calculation. Then we ask the program to run on a real computer and no longer on a software simulator.

```
from qiskit import ClassicalRegister,
QuantumRegister, QuantumCircuit
from qiskit import execute
from qiskit import IBMQ
IBMQ.load_accounts()
from qiskit.providers.ibmq import
least_busy
large_enough_devices =
IBMQ.backends(filters=lambda x:
x.configuration().n_qubits > 3 and not
x.configuration().simulator)
backend = least_busy(large_enough_devices)
print("The best backend is " +
backend.name())
print("Real Quantum Computer !")
q = QuantumRegister(3)
c = ClassicalRegister(3)
circuit = QuantumCircuit(q, c)
circuit.h(q[0])
circuit.h(q[1])
circuit.h(q[2])
circuit.measure(q, c)
job = execute(circuit, backend, shots=100,
max_credits=3)
print(job.result().get_counts(circuit))
```

Here is the result :

```
The best backend is ibmqx4
Real Quantum Computer !
{'011': 14, '101': 12, '000': 19, '100':
11, '010': 13, '111': 5, '110': 10, '001':
16}
```

You have now seen your first quantum program run on a real quantum computer.

IBM also provides a complex simulator of quantum computer that emulates the real conditions (noise, decoherence, etc.).

SUMMARY

- ✓ YOU CAN TODAY ACCESS TO REAL QUANTUM COMPUTERS ON THE CLOUD.

- ✓ VENDORS PROVIDE QUANTUM COMPUTER SIMULATORS, FROM VERY BASIC TO MORE ADVANCED FEATURES (NOISE, DECORRELATION, ETC.).

- ✓ PYTHON HAS BECOME THE MOST USED LANGUAGE FOR BEGINNING IN QUANTUM PROGRAMMING.

8.   MOORE'S LAW AND QUANTUM

The famous *Moore's Law* is a empiric but foundation law of modern electronics and computers.

Gordon Moore, a giant in the history of computing and co-founder of Fairchild and Intel, told in the 60s that the number of components (the famous transistors, basic elements of microprocessors) would double each year with equivalent area on the chip.

One can also say that computing power would double each year at same equivalent cost. This is not really a demonstrable scientific law but rather a vision that has been true until today, despite all the technological issues researchers had to fix.

We can underline that this law, which is linear and impressive, does less well than other equivalent but exponential laws, such as the development of networks and mobile phones and genome sequencing technologies [5].

Currently, there is a theoretical limit to the evolution of Moore's Law. Indeed, below 5 nm (nanometers), it is no longer possible to reduce the size of transistors due to quantum effect, precisely (*tunneling*)!

Does Moore's Law apply to Quantum Computing?

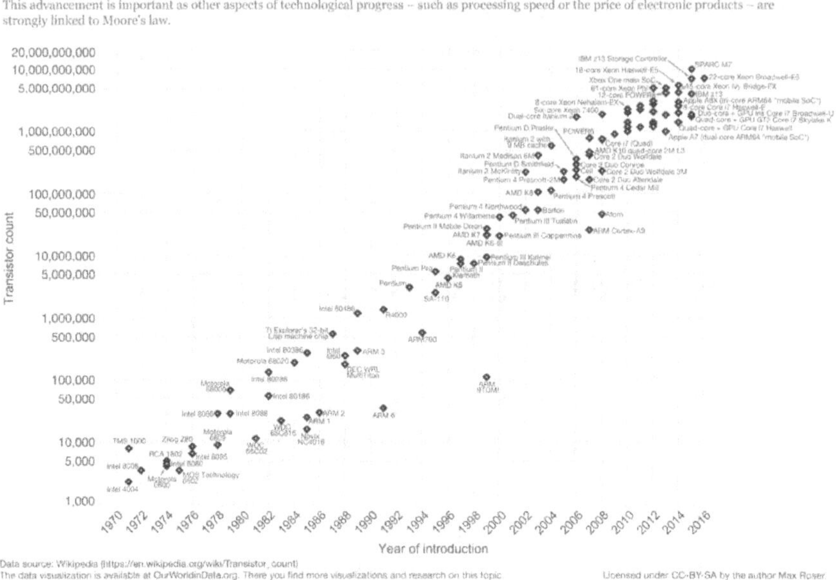

Figure 12: Moore's Law – number of transistors over time

It began in 1960 with a paper written by the Israeli physicist Stephen Wiesner who proposed an anti-fraud system in the banking domain using the transmission of two messages whose reading of one destroyed the other. But his works were too new for the time and were not recognized until ten years later.

In 1973, Russian Soviet mathematician Alexander Holevo [6] demonstrated a fundamental theorem of Quantum Computing (the now famous Holevo's Theorem). This theorem establishes that n qubits cannot *carry* more than n conventional bits of information. It is very surprising since I mentioned several times in this book that Quantum Computing is much better than Classical Computing. I refer the readers who want to understand this particular paradigm to read the last Chapter regarding the Mathematics behind Quantum.

The Polish physicist Roman Stanislaw Ingarden [7] opened the quantum Pandora box in 1976 by proposing to generalize Shannon's Theorem to Quantum Physics. Shannon's theorem is one of the basic principles of information theory.

In May 1981, during a conference at MIT, Richard Feynman stated that it seemed impossible to simulate the evolution of a quantum system effectively on a conventional computer. He then proposed a basic model to make this type of simulations [8].

In 1984, the first quasi-founding element of Quantum Computing was established, the famous BB84 protocol of Charles Bennett and Gilles Brassard [9]. It described how to securely exchange a private encryption key using the properties of Quantum Physics. Both researchers are considered as the founding fathers of Quantum Computing. Charles Bennett is in particular the author of the "4 laws of quantum information theory".

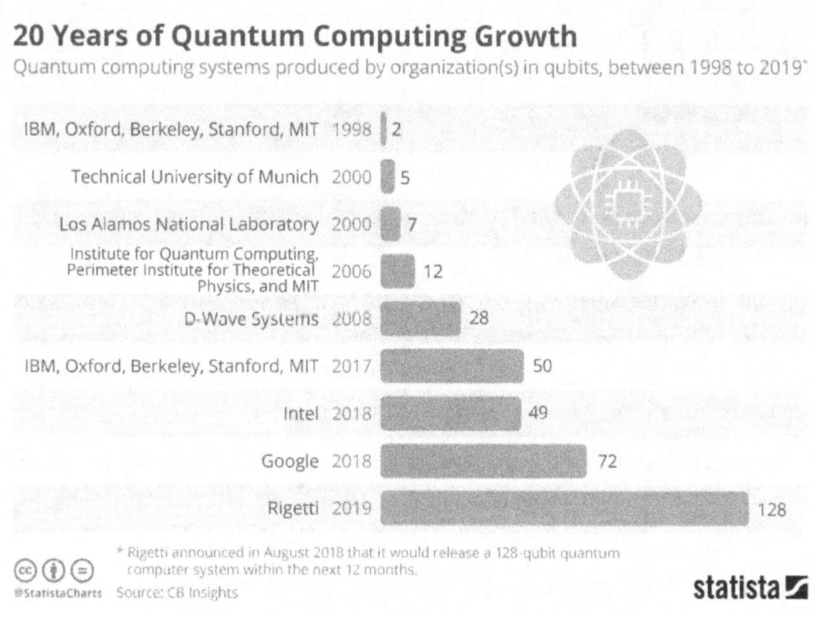

Figure 13: 20 years of Quantum Computing Growth

Ten years after, Peter Shor brought a new founding stone with its famous algorithm. In essence, Shor demonstrated that a quantum computer could theoretically break any cryptographic algorithm based on the factorization of large numbers, which is the basis of modern cryptography.

IBM has proposed a new method of measuring the progress of Quantum Computing, a kind of equivalence of Moore's Law, the **Quantum Volume**.

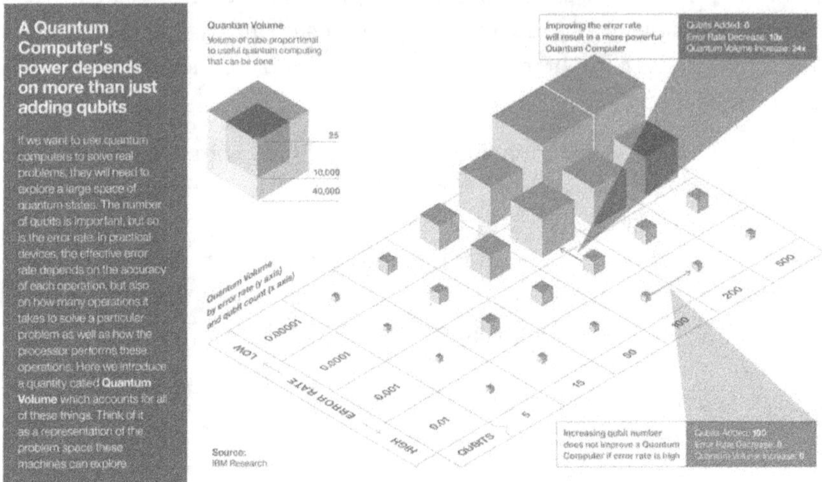

Figure 14: Quantum Volume

This measurement is defined by the number of qubits, the error rates and the connectivity between qubits.

Basically this definition means that it is not enough to add qubits to a quantum computer to improve its performance. A quantum computer is extremely sensitive to any disturbance (vibration, waves, temperature variations) which may lead to computation errors.

If this calculation method is applied to IBM's own quantum systems, we find an evolution similar to Moore's Law from 2017 to 2019 (respectively, 4, 8 and 16).

As a matter of fact, quantum algorithms evolve very quickly.

In 2019, the company ProteinQure, which is specialized in quantum computing and Machine Learning in the pharmaceutical field, introduced an interesting concept: **Quantum Value**. It proposed to balance two concepts:

- The Quantum Value which improves how to solve a problem using a quantum computer (or a combination with a conventional computer) and to achieve better results than with a conventional solution. Improvement stands less in the speed of execution than in more convincing results.

- The Quantum Advantage which allows to solve a problem with a quantum computer faster, cheaper or more efficiently than with a conventional computer.

The concept of Quantum Valuation is relevant because the technological (and probably financial) barrier to entry is much lower. It works when the error type of the quantum algorithm is different (uncorrelated) from the error type of the classical algorithm.

Another (surprising) way to express this concept is that the quantum algorithm does not necessarily have to be better. It just has to make mistakes (the famous rate of errors) differently than the classic algorithm. This means that the concept will be relevant only to certain classes of problems that match to this specificity.

Consider the following example which is a known problem in Artificial Intelligence, so-called classification.

Let's take a set of 1 million so-cute dog pictures. Among these images, hundred nasty cats have infiltrated. Our mission is to sort these images and delete the images of cats.

In classical computer science, we would use an Artificial Intelligence algorithm of the Deep Learning Classifier type. Once we have applied the algorithm, although powerful, it would have only identified for example 90 images of cats. It has missed 10 cats, so-called *false negatives*. It is assumed that the algorithm did not take dogs for cats, which would be *false positives*.

Now let's use a quantum algorithm. Imagine that this algorithm would only find 12 cats and that therefore seems less efficient, except that only 7 of these cats have already been found by the classical algorithm. This means that the quantum algorithm found 5 cats that the classical algorithm would never have found.

The use of the two algorithms makes it possible to find 95 cats and halve the false negative rate. That is Quantum Valuation!

By the way, be sure that quantum solutions vendors will compete in the coming years and that the volume of press releases will follow Moore's Law and double each year!

SUMMARY

- ✓ MOORE'S LAW STATES THAT THE COMPUTING POWER WILL DOUBLE EVERY YEAR AT THE SAME COST IN CLASSICAL COMPUTING.

- ✓ IN QUANTUM COMPUTING, THE NUMBER OF QUBITS (AS THE NUMBER OF TRANSISTORS IN CLASSICAL COMPUTING) IS NOT A COMPLETE INDEX OF COMPUTING POWER. OTHER PARAMETERS HAVE TO BE INCLUDED.

- ✓ ALGORITHM QUALITY IS AS MUCH AS IMPORTANT AS QUBITS QUALITY.

- ✓ RESEARCHERS HAVE TO HYBRIDIZE CLASSICAL COMPUTING AND QUANTUM COMPUTING.

9.   DOES QUANTUM KILL CRYPTOGRAPHY?

We often read or hear that Quantum Computing will strongly impact certain activities such as financial transactions or e-commerce because no cryptography could resist it.

In May 2018, during a meeting of The Churchill Club in San Francisco, Arvind Krishna, director of IBM Research, announced that: "*Anyone wishing to protect its data for the next 10 years must switch to post-quantum cryptography*". It was a loud and clear message: in 10 years, Quantum Computing would be able to break all the current cryptography.

Cryptography combines mathematical algorithms and processes to protect the confidentiality, integrity and authentication of data that we call messages [10]. Just like the secret messages you probably sent to your friends or lover during your highschool years using ink made of lemon juice.

Some experts even speak of *post-quantum cryptography* to emphasize that there would be one cryptography *before* and one cryptography *after* the advent of Quantum Computing.

Urban legend or true paradigm shift? Let's try to elaborate a bit further.

First of all, there should be no confusion between quantum cryptography and post-quantum cryptography. **Quantum cryptography** uses quantum phenomena. **Post-quantum cryptography**, by misuse of language, refers to cryptographic algorithms that cannot be solved much faster by a quantum computer than by a conventional computer.

Please let me begin with a little reminder about (classical) cryptography.

There are 3 main families of cryptographic algorithms and applications:

- Hashing functions : They can generate a kind of signature, a virtual hallmark or seal to guarantee and challenge the integrity of a file, for example. When you download a large file on a Dropbox-type service, you can use this technology to verify that the downloaded file is right. Certificates and electronic signatures also exploit these features. For example: MD5, SHA-1, SHA-2.

- Symmetric encryption: The oldest technique of cryptographers, often called '*by secret key*', and used in all good old spy movies. In essence, symmetric cryptography has existed since Humanity needs to protect private or sensible information. As a drawback, one must first find a way to secretly distribute the (secret) key to those who want to exchange securely information. Then, the sender can encrypt with the secret key and the receiver can decipher with this same key. This technology is very efficient in terms of computing power and memory requirements. By cons, it requires the exchange of the secret key with all the potential disadvantages: loss, theft, misuse for compromise, etc. For example: DES, 3DES, AES.

- Asymmetric encryption: This technique, from the 70s, often called '*by public key*', avoids the exchange of the secret key made necessary with symmetric encryption. On the other hand, it consumes computing time and memory because it uses the factorization of integers or logarithmic calculations. It has revolutionized and still revolutionizes our lives every day: e-commerce, crypto-currencies, PGP, etc. For example: RSA, elliptic curves.

In general, a cryptosystem uses several types of cryptography. For example asymmetric encryption can be used to secretly exchange the private keys of the symmetric encryption, which will then actually encrypt the data.

Asymmetric cryptography is based on the factorization of large integers into prime numbers. Prime numbers are mathematical objects that have very particular properties. These are integers that are only divisible by 1 and by themselves. They are therefore all odd, except 2 which is the only even prime number. Any integer can be broken down into prime numbers. This process is named *factorization*.

For example:

$12 = 2$ x 2 x 3 ; which can be written: 2^2 x 3

$457 = 457$ (457 is a prime number)

$458 = 2$ x 229

$459 = 3^3$ x 17

If we consider two prime numbers of large size (for example of 250 digits each) and multiply them, it becomes almost impossible to achieve the reverse calculation (a factorization in prime numbers), even for an extremely powerful computer. This particularity of non-reversibility of computation is at the base of symmetric cryptography.

In 1994, Peter Shor, then professor at MIT, developed a quantum algorithm able to factorize integers faster than with a conventional computer. The quantum computation time to factorize became polynomial with the number of digits and no longer exponential. This discovery convinced some researchers it would be possible to break - theoretically at least - many asymmetric cryptographies, known as public keys cryptographies.

However, at the technical implementation level, this discovery needs that quantum computer may store and process very large integers which is far from being true at the moment.

In 1996, Grover proposed a new quantum algorithm that could efficiently search for items in an unordered list or unstructured database. This algorithm makes it possible to speed up the search for a certain type of encryption key (symmetric encryption). Indeed, the time needed to break the cryptography by brute force (trying all combinations), is only $2^{n/2}$ iterations instead of 2^n in classical computing.

Since then, the concept of post-quantum cryptography has been introduced by the National Institute of Standards and Technology (NIST) to designate any algorithm that can withstand Shor's Algorithm.

This new class of algorithms now exists in two categories: the most interesting algorithms are considered unbreakable by mathematical proof (*formal proof*), the others are considered sufficiently resistant in terms of the number of qubits and decryption time which are required to break them.

For example, it has been mathematically proven that the Lattice algorithm class is resistant to quantum computers. No algorithm known to date can break this type of cryptography.

In the case of symmetric cryptography, in the current state of knowledge, it is possible to keep using the current algorithms if the size of the encryption keys is increased. For example, for the widely used AES algorithm, doubling the key size from 256 bits to 512 bits may be acceptable.

Still in the current state of knowledge, hash functions are not impacted by Quantum Computing (although there have recently been many flaws detected and exploitable by classical computing).

By the way, '*state of knowledge*' is a fuzzy term because nobody knows what governmental agencies actually know…

Consider that we want to evaluate the resistance of a *message* with encryption, which means encrypted using a cryptographic algorithm. We must immediately take into account the creation date of the encrypted message. There are three cases:

- The message was encrypted a long time ago (about ten years ago). There is a good chance that the algorithm used has already been weakened or broken. It is also possible that the current computing power - classical computing - can decipher it by brute force. The brute force process can decipher by trying all the possible combinations, which can take a few minutes to a few years. Remember for example the breaking of the passwords of the first generation of Wi-Fi networks which exploited a weakness of the algorithm allowing the attacks by brute force.

- The message is encrypted today. The choice of the cryptographic algorithm and the size of the key should be done according to the requested level of confidentiality and integrity but also the availability of local encryption/decryption tools. Most current algorithms, if properly implemented, help ensure a high level of security for many years to come. However, in twenty years, when quantum computers have evolved, message will most likely be breakable.

- The message will be created and encrypted in the more or less close future. It seems clear that post-quantum cryptography will become the *de facto* standard. As any technological innovation, demanding and costly, it is likely that it will be limited initially for applications requiring a high, persistent and guaranteed level of security.

The advent of a quantum computer with sufficient capacity for threatening classical cryptography is still distant. In the meantime, we can think that research on post-quantum cryptography will be well advanced, and that the change in cryptographic paradigm can be widely anticipated.

QUANTUM KEY DISTRIBUTION

Quantum Key Distribution (QKD) is one of the main and most promising applications of Quantum Physics, thanks to qubits entanglement. In a previous chapter, we have learned that the reading (measurement) of the state of one of the entangled qubits irremediably leads to the loss (collapse) of information on the other qubit. Theoretically this property should allow to detect any attempt to read a quantum encryption key by a third party. Here is the famous BB84 Protocol born in 1984.

This protocol is often misunderstood.

We have seen that the main problem of symmetric cryptography was the distribution of the private key to only those authorized to encrypt and decrypt messages. If the key is stolen or intercepted by a third party, the latter can decrypt the messages but can also encrypt fakes, without the knowledge of authorized persons. For example, during the Second World War, the Germans ignored for a long time that the Allies broke their Enigma system and could read their secret messages.

In classical cryptography, we can use public-key asymmetric cryptography to securely exchange the private and secret keys of symmetric cryptography that will be used to encrypt messages. However, for some extremely private communications, you'd better not use asymmetric cryptography for private key distribution.

BB84 Protocol was proposed in 1984 by Charles H. Bennett, IBM T.J. Watson Research Center, and Gilles Brassard, Montréal University.

A photon can be polarized along two axes (or bases): H: Horizontal (0) or V: Vertical (Pi/2) and A: Antidiagonal (Pi/4) or D: Diagonal (3pi/4). The fictitious graphical angles are in parentheses for your better understanding.

Consider arbitrarily that the polarizations V and D represent the information bit '1', and respectively H and A, the information bit '0'.

The sender will send to the receiver a series of photons polarized randomly along the rectilinear and diagonal axes (H, V, A or D). This transmission is done via a quantum communication link, usually by optical fiber.

In Cryptography, we like to personalize the roles of the sender and receiver. It is common to name Alice the sender of a message and Bob the recipient.

We also introduce the (wicked) Eve who will try to intercept the messages between Alice and Bob (love affair?).

The recipient will receive this sequence (with some photons lost due to defects in the transmission and/or the detector) and will measure their polarization along an axis (rectilinear or diagonal) randomly chosen for each photon.

Once all the measurements have been done, the recipient will use an unsecured communication channel such as the Internet to inform the sender of the measurement axis he has used for each photon.

The sender compares this information with his own polarization choices and informs the recipient of which results are correct.

The sender and the receiver compare their results and reject all the results the recipient was wrong (the recipient did not measure with the correct axis) or if the photon was lost.

```
To represent the polarizations of photons, we use the
following symbols :

+    rectilinear
O    diagonal

To represent the measurements :

<    anti-diagonal
>    diagonal
|    vertical
-    horizontal

Example of transmission and data exchange :

Alice sends a sequence of 32 photons polarized randomly:

><><>|-<|-|--|><><<>><||<<>>|-<|>

Bob measures each photon according to randomly chosen axes:

+++++O+O+O+O+O+O+++++++O+OOOO+O+

And reads (with some lost photons) :

||--|  -<|  |>-<|<-||-  |<->>< -> |

Bob tells to Alice his bases of measurement (mentioning lost
photons) via a traditional communication channel :

+++++ +O+ +O+O+O++++ +O+OOO +O +

Alice answers him:

 -<.|. < .<.. |

Bob answers :

 -<.|. < .<.. |

The system has not been compromised!
```

Figure 15: Example of Quantum Key Distribution BB84 Protocol

To spy Alice and Bob, Eve must intercept the photons sent by Alice, then, for each photon, measure its polarization along one of the axes, rectilinear or diagonal. But especially, knowing that the measurement may change the photon state, she must forward a new polarized photon for each intercepted photon.

Unfortunately for Eve, she does not know the axis chosen by Alice for each photon. Since she can measure the intercepted photon only on one axis and it is impossible to copy a photon (Heisenberg's uncertainty principle), it means that chances are she is wrong by sending back the photon with the wrong polarization. As Bob has also a chance over 2 not to select the right axe, Eve will be wrong once in four.

To summarize:

- If the communication has not been eavesdropped by Eve or a third party, the probability of a correct measurement is 3/4 (that is, 1/2 * (1 + 1/2)).

- If, on the other hand, Eve has intercepted the message, the probability is 5/8 (that is, 1/2 * (3/4 + 1/2)).

The sender and the recipient may understand that they have been eavesdropped if the result does not match the right probability.

If they have been eavesdropped, they just have to repeat the process.

If the transmission has been secure, part of the information transmitted by the quantum channel may become the secret private key.

In 1989, the two researchers validated their theory by achieving QKD practically over a distance of 32 cm.

The advanced reader may have perhaps noted that this protocol is only valid if Eve does not pretend to be Bob to Alice. So Alice and Bob should authenticate each other first!

In 1991, Ekert published a secret key distribution protocol based on the Bell's theorem.

In March 2019, Singaporean company SK Telecom announced its first Quantum Security Gateway, intended to be installed in communicating (and possibly autonomous) cars to protect all vehicle systems and all communications. This security would be provided by a quantum random number generator and quantum distribution of encryption keys. As a reminder, in 2018, SK Telecom took a majority stake in the Swiss start-up Quantum ID, which for several years had been protecting sensitive networks such as those between two banking datacenters.

The first quantum cryptography systems appeared at the beginning of the 2000s. Some systems were broken or weakened but as usual in this domain, they were eventually defects of hardware or wrong software implementations. Quantum principles have never been questioned. Some protocols were also biased by design.

The researchers have then developed cryptographic protocols independent of the hardware. In early 2019, Chinese scientists successfully attacked these new protocols. A complicated story of laser resonance, but the same researchers found the countermeasure.

SUMMARY

- ✓ QUANTUM COMPUTING CAN POTENTIALLY BREAK SOME CIPHERING ALGORITHMS BUT QUANTUM COMPUTERS THAT CAN ACHIEVE THESE TASKS WON'T BE AVAILABLE BEFORE SEVERAL YEARS

- ✓ SOME EXISTING CRYPTOGRAPHIC ALGORITHMS CANNOT BE BROKEN BY QUANTUM COMPUTING.

- ✓ IT'S POSSIBLE TO DISTRIBUTE CIPHERING KEYS IN FULL SECURE PROCESS USING QUANTUM KEY DISTRIBUTION.

10.   WHAT IMPACT ON ARTIFICIAL INTELLIGENCE?

It is unlikely that you miss the current buzz on Artificial Intelligence (AI). This is a little ice on cake of any new IT project or startup at the moment.

As a matter of fact, there has not been a real revolution in Artificial Intelligence. The author of these lines even graduated in Artificial Intelligence in 1988! Except for last years, he had always avoided mentioning this expertise in his CV, because AI guys were like black sheeps. His first network of 4 neurons had been programmed on Excel (I swear it's true!) then in LISP (an interesting language but since fallen into oblivion).

The real revolution in AI is due to the advent of GPU parallel computing cards (these same graphics cards you buy to play on your computer) and the availability of plenty of cheap enough computing power on the Cloud. It has hence become possible to run these good old AI algorithms with large data sets and huge neural networks.

Experts has probably frown and thought that it is a very simplifying vision but I assume. However, I must confess many theoretical and technological developments were made in AI in the 2010s.

So, regarding AI, I talked about parallel computing, large numbers of neurons and large volumes of data. That sounds very similar to the benefits of Quantum Computing. Could quantum technology change AI?

In Computer Science, it's all about Mathematics and algorithms.

In AI, most algorithms are based on solving a particular type of equations: linear equations or rather a system of several linear equations. Mathematics of linear equations have been well known for centuries and conventional computers have effective algorithms to solve them.

Problem is the classical computing calculation time to solve these linear equations is proportional *exponentially* to the number of unknowns.

In 2008, the term *Quantum Machine Learning* became a reality thanks to Aram Harrow, Avinatan Hassidim and Seth Lloyd and their famous revolutionary algorithm HHL [10].

This algorithm promised a quantum resolution time no more exponential but *logarithmic*, which has been a huge gain as soon as the number of unknowns is high like in IA.

This algorithm is still used as a base for new algorithms, especially in Supervised Machine Learning, a domain of AI. Google would use it to calculate some properties of its famous PageRank algorithm.

Quantum Computing is particularly suitable for shape or pattern recognition, one of the application fields of AI. In 2016, California researchers used a 1152-qubit D-Wave 2X computer to analyze hundreds of satellite images of California. The goal was to detect certain types of trees by assisted vision and shape recognition. The results obtained with quantum computing were more accurate than with a conventional computer.

However, it is necessary to balance all the enthusiasm around this algorithm and its derivatives. Indeed, a careful reading of the practical conditions of implementation made by several experts moderates the time saving. The requirements are fairly restrictive and as usual in Quantum Computing, only a probability of result is measured at once (so we must repeat several times the same calculation and measurement).

In January 2019, a new step had been achieved: teams from IBM's JT Watson Research Center in the United States announced that for the very first time a quantum computer had learned to recognize a form in Supervised Machine Learning.

Computations in Artificial Intelligence require thousands of qubits. Several start-ups and researchers are currently working on quantum algorithms specific to Artificial Intelligence. But the technological leap will be a reality only when quantum computers have evolved in terms of the number and stability (coherence time) of qubits.

SUMMARY

- ✓ QUANTUM COMPUTING AND ARTIFICIAL INTELLIGENCE FIT WELL.

- ✓ SOME COMPANIES USE BOTH CLASSICAL AND QUANTUM COMPUTING TO OPTIMIZE SOME KINDS OF COMPUTATION IN AI.

- ✓ IN 2019, THERE ARE NOT ENOUGH QUBITS IN AVAILABLE QUANTUM COMPUTERS TO PROVIDE A MAJOR TECHNOLOGICAL LEAP IN AI.

11.   QUANTUM REVOLUTION: TRUTH OR LIE?

I agree that the title of this chapter is a little bit provocative. Nevertheless, this is the phrase that I heard during one of my quantum computing seminars in France in 2018. Definitely sceptic people. I'm an ethical professional so I won't disclose the customer company name. I interrupted my presentation and showed on the screen the execution of a program in Python on a quantum computer available in the Cloud. A simple program, a simulation of coin tossing game, but on a real quantum computer with 4 qubits. I also noted that the service provider provided a 16-qubit computer.

It reminded me a meeting in 1999 with the strategy head of a large telecom operator when I was told that Video on Demand (VoD) had no future. No kidding...

So, Quantum Computing, truth or lie? For sure, the world may not be revolutionized with the quantum simulation of a coin flipping. I usually answer with a joke (a quantum one!): Quantum Computing is currently simultaneously both truth and lie.

At the dawn of the 2020s, Quantum Computing industry is still very far from bringing to the market computers with thousands of logical qubits (or millions of physical qubits) that we would need to revolutionize the world.

On another hand, the quantum developer is still a rare species, hard to hunt. Training and academic courses are scarce, job position opportunities too, and service companies and system integrators are not yet interested. But that will probably change quickly.

Like any technological revolution, the first users has been high-income or high-value-added industries such as GAFAM and their Chinese equivalents, BATX, the financial sector, the pharmaceutical industry, the chemistry sector. It's not tomorrow that everyone will have a quantum computer at home, but no one today has a HPC-type supercomputer at home as well.

Please let me go back in 1968 to remind you of a great moment in forgotten computer science history. On December 9, 1968, Mr. Doug Engelbart of Stanford University, who should be known today as well as Steve Jobs, video-recorded a near-revolutionary public demonstration of what Computer Science was about to become. At that time the public hardly knew what a computer was: a pile of cabinets in air-conditioned rooms with flashing lights, card readers and teleprinters. In this demonstration, now known as *"Mother of all demos"*, Engelbart used the first mouse, used a graphical interface, windows whose size it changed with the mouse, hypertext links on which he pointed, videoconferencing, collaborative processing and word processing. Just *only* that!

As a great visionary, he even spoke of *augmented* human through computer science.

Why has I quoted Engelbart and his demonstration? Because in Quantum Computing, we are at the same stage roughly speaking. The key concepts are known but we are still stammering.

The first prototypes of quantum computers appeared in the early 2000s. Since 2010, companies like D-Wave, Rigetti Computing, IonQ, IBM or Google make periodic announcements and already provide access to their machines via the Cloud.

Europe is not the last in this technological race with leading companies like Atos which provides quantum simulators. These simulators allow testing and optimization of quantum algorithms for future uses in real conditions (noise, decoherence, etc.). Dutch University of Delft is also a quick and efficient doer and mover in Quantum Computer Architecture and Quantum Internet.

In 2001, an IBM team demonstrated that it was possible to use the Shor's Algorithm to factorize the number $15 = 3 \times 5$, using a 7-qubit computer (NMR / NMR nuclear magnetic resonance technology). It was a kind of *"Mother of all quantum demos"*.

Then, another team achieved the same calculation but with qubits with photons. It was not until 2012 to get the same result with qubits with ion traps and to manage to factorize 21.

In April 2012, a new record was set with the factorization of 143 = 11 x 13 with a different algorithm, which allowed in 2014 to factor 56153 = 233 x 241.

D-Wave, funded with $200 million, announced a platform of 5000 qubits in 2020, compared to the 2000 qubits of its own technology in 2018. The number may seem impressive but the qubits of D-Wave are not the same as those of its competitors IBM, Rigetti or Google. Their coherence time is much lower by technological choice and the quantum computer is designed to solve particular problems. It is interesting to note that this company is also making a jump in interconnections, from 6 to 15 interconnections between qubits.

On another hand, IonQ proved in March 2019 that its quantum system solved complex problems much more efficiently than a conventional computer using brute force for this type of problem (Bernstein-Vazirani and Hidden Shift algorithms, respectively). 78% and 35% at the first test for the computer of IonQ against 0.1% for a conventional computer). It had been a concrete and convincing result that opened serious horizons for quantum computation.

At the time of writing (2019), the most powerful quantum computer integrates 128 qubits (Rigetti Computing) and has a limited number of instructions but addressable in advanced languages such as C++ or Python. The experts agree that the paradigm shift will be a reality when one will be able to build a quantum processor with millions of physical qubits, just as the industry knows how to do it in traditional computing.

Future is bright but the road is still long.

12.   WILL MY BUSINESS BE IMPACTED?

If we listen to the most optimistic futurologists, Quantum Computing should be a revolution superior to the arrival of the Internet. For the most pessimistic critics, who boast of realism, it would be a wet firecracker that will only slightly impact our society by an extremely limited scope.

It is difficult at the moment to balance. There are three key points : smart people and smart money are interested by the Quantum topic, research is accelerating and two axes of improvement are currently very attractive (algorithms and error correction).

Algorithmics can find ways to calculate faster and more efficiently with Quantum. In general, Quantum gain comes from a linear or logarithmic calculation time instead of an exponential calculation time. Sometimes it's not possible to go beyond the exponential simplification but there may be still a quantum technological advantage for some calculations.

The error correction, whether at the level of physical or logical qubits, architecture, inter-qubit communication or programming, makes it possible to increase the power of a quantum computer (optimization of the coherence time included).

It is probably on these two axes that everything will happen in the next five years.

The point is that most large technology companies invest heavily in Quantum, followed, admittedly a little behind, by the states, including Europe.

Applications are already numerous and promising:

- Quantum Internet: True promise to get a secure Internet, it will interconnect major cities, sensitive networks of companies or critical infrastructure operators.

- Quantum atomic clocks: These extremely stable and precise clocks make it possible, for example, to optimize the operation of GPS, to guarantee the synchronization of energy networks (the famous Grid) or complex telecommunications systems.

- Quantum sensors: The superposition state of qubits is extremely sensitive to environment, which makes it possible to use it as a sensor, for example of very weak magnetic fields, or as a particle detector. Interferometry can also benefit from Quantum. Several applications seem also to emerge both in medicine for non-invasive analysis and for the detection of certain minerals under the ground.

- Quantum simulators: We don't talk there about a classical computer that simulates a quantum computer but about a quantum computer that simulates complex systems at the quantum level, such as atomic or molecular interactions or properties in biomolecular chemistry.

We have already introduced the Quantum impacts on Cryptography and Artificial Intelligence in terms of intrinsic technologies.

Let's move on to the application side, by sector of business.

Design of a new molecule, for the pharmaceutical or chemical domains, is often quoted as primary quantum application. The quantum computer makes it possible to simulate all the positions of all the atoms of the new molecule, even before it can be synthesized. Companies have even specialized in this field: Qulab, ProteinQure, Heisenberg or even Entropica Labs that works in genetic analysis.

Financial engineering will also be deeply impacted. Quantum Computing, coupled with Artificial Intelligence, can find the best combination of securities in a portfolio of 100 or more securities, with periodic arbitrage. According to JP Morgan Chase, even its best traders are no better at this optimization game. QxBranch is one of the active players in this sector.

LOGISTICS & SUPPLY CHAIN

The promoters of Quantum Computing often talk about the resolution of problems of optimal path finding, or so-called *traveling salesman problem*. The problem is for example the calculation of the optimal path of a salesman in several dozens of cities by taking into account several factors, called constraints, such as gas mileage, the number of kilometers traveled in total, the number of spent hotel nights, etc.

This is a class of well-known problems in logistics. Quantum Computing associated with Artificial Intelligence could excel and bring significant productivity gains. However, to be relevant in real cases, the quantum computer needs several thousand qubits.

MEDICINE

Once again, the alliance between Artificial Intelligence (at least its algorithms) and Quantum Computing can be decisive. Several studies are currently carried out in the research or diagnosis of cancers or the behavior of the human body against certain molecules, in order to customize treatments.

Several start-ups also work on optimizing MRI (Magnetic Resonance Imaging) techniques by improving magnetic field sensor sensitivity and measurement accuracy.

CLIMATOLOGY

Meteorology and more generally climatology are among the biggest users of high performance computers (HPC). It is therefore normal for these disciplines turn to Quantum Computing, whose bestiary of algorithms corresponds fairly well to their problematic.

Currently, researchers are focusing on models of climate change, a real social issue.

AUTOMOTIVE

In May 2019, at the Lisbon Web Summit, Volkswagen and D-Wave surprised all attendees by proposing a real-time prediction application for road traffic based on a quantum computer. Promising a reduction in traffic jams, accidents and pollution, it was the result of a partnership of more than two years between the two companies.

Volkswagen is not the only car manufacturer to be interested in Quantum Computing. Ford has a dedicated team that works closely with its Artificial Intelligence teams and with NASA. Bosch has partnered with Harvard

University's Zapata Computing spin-off. Japanese equipment manufacturer Denso uses Quantum Computing to optimize the movements of its automated vehicles.

Improvement of energy storage capacity, size and weight of electric vehicle batteries, is another current challenge of the automotive industry. Daimler, IBM and Google are working in partnership on the atomic level modeling of the constituents of these batteries such as Lithium.

NAVIGATION

The quantum principle of superposition is extremely sensitive to magnetic fields. Researchers try to exploit this feature to develop a new type of accelerometer that could replace a GPS system when not usable (for example in underwater environment).

Another example, in France, the Laboratory of Digital Photonics and Nanosciences has associated a quantum accelerometer with a conventional accelerometer to perform a very precise differential measurement.

SEISMOLOGY

On the same theoretical concepts, it is possible to develop a quantum gravimeter that detects deeply buried objects or changes in the Earth's gravitational field. A gravimeter is in fact a type of very sensitive accelerometer specialized in the measurement of a vertical acceleration close to gravity.

UK-based start-up QuantIC works on a portable system that could better predict tsunamis and earthquakes.

PHARMACEUTICAL INDUSTRY

Closely related to chemistry, pharmaceutical industry is probably the most concerned and impacted business domain by the quantum revolution.

Many companies, like start-up 1QBit, are working on the design of specialized algorithms, mixing Quantum and Machine Learning.

They search for new antibodies at the molecular level, simulate the folding of proteins (that is essential to understand how they work) or create immune system models.

Applications in the search for new drugs are numerous with huge return on investment opportunities: Alzheimer's disease, multiple sclerosis, cancers, etc.

PHYSICS

In his founding speech in 1981, the famous professor Richard Feynman suggested that the only way to build a simulation of the physical world at the quantum level was to use a quantum machine.

Physicists are therefore the first interested in Quantum Computing to verify hypotheses or perform complex calculations which are impossible to achieve with a conventional computer.

CHEMISTRY

Chemists dream of being able to simulate the functioning of complex molecules such as proteins. Even the most powerful classical computers are not always able to do it.

A quantum computer is the best candidate to compute or simulate quantum effects at the intramolecular level.

However, even though the research is currently promising, quantum computers do not yet have the size, in terms of number of qubits, to perform this kind of calculation.

Volkswagen automaker and quantum computer manufacturer D-Wave are collaborating in the search for new materials using Quantum Computing. In 2019, they presented encouraging results (albeit quite limited at the moment) in the search for the energy states of a hybrid of hydrogen and lithium molecules.

Both molecules are well known by chemists. IBM had already worked on this subject in 2017 with quantum calculations but the use of D-Wave technology is an interesting advance.

Volkswagen expects to be able to use future D-Wave quantum computers to design next-generation electric car batteries, optimized solar panels and research on new materials.

Business cases are numerous in this domain and with high level of return on investment.

VIDEO GAMING

The video game industry is now a major sector of entertainment with a global turnover of almost 50 billion in 2017.

It could benefit from Quantum Computing on several aspects: optimization of the engines that manage the physics of solids (for example the simulation of an object that falls and breaks), NPC (Non Player Characters) and smarter bots (in coupling with Artificial Intelligence), but also optimization of sports betting systems in real time and most importantly, alas, potential ability to cheat on some online games, such as poker.

In parallel, researchers in Artificial Intelligence continue their quest for the Machine against the Human: Chess, Go, Magic: The Assembly (Gathering), etc. They will probably use the algorithmic specificities of Quantum Computing to solve this type of problem.

SUMMARY

- ✓ MOST BUSINESSES WILL BE CONCERNED AND IMPACTED.

- ✓ CURRENTLY, THERE ARE ONLY PROOFS OF CONCEPT (PoCs) AND BUSINESS CASES.

- ✓ FOR ACTUAL IMPACT ON DAY-TO-DAY BUSINESS, IT WOULD NEED QUANTUM COMPUTERS WITH THOUSAND OR MILLIONS OF INTERCONNECTED QUBITS.

13.   I WANT TO FOUND MY QUANTUM START-UP!

In a very relevant paper (Le Monde, March 26th, 2019 [11]), Charles Beigbeder and Christophe Jurczak, pleaded for a necessary French and European public policy of Physics and Quantum Computing.

There are already dozens of start-ups in Quantum Computing. The best known is probably Rigetti Computing, named from its founder. IonQ is also particularly quotable thanks to the mastering of its technology and the pragmatic and concrete results of its work on algorithms.

Alongside the behemoths like IBM or Google, quantum start-ups try to find a place in this emerging market, thanks to their choices and their technological innovations. In Quantum Computing, size is probably an even more dramatic and decisive advantage than in Artificial Intelligence. Just think about the amount of required investment, the brains to attract and the quite far return on investment (ROI). Remember however that Rigetti has already raised $120M for its development.

Quantum start-ups must also make strategic alliances necessary to survive against their competitors, some of them with enormous financial means. For example, Rigetti has partnered with Amazon and its AWS Cloud to build its Quantum Cloud Services in order to compete with IBM.

There are also dedicated incubators like the famous Creative Destruction Lab at Toronto, Canada.

That reminds me a Dilbert© comics quote: *"The project exists in a simultaneous state of being both totally successful and not even started"*. This can apply to any startup or Quantum Computing project. Or both.

In my career, I had the opportunity to participate in a lot of due diligences of start-up or buyout financing transactions. And also, conversely, to find myself in the seat, often not very comfortable, of the CEO of the start-up or of the acquired company. Apart from a few investment funds that really know the technologies (see the preface by Charles Beigbeder of Quantonation) and of course those who are my customers (*smile*), many VCs behave like sheep. No offense, only business. You just have, according to the seasons and the years, to include some magic words in your pitch or your deck: blockchain (which is however not so very fashionable anymore...), IoT, Artificial Intelligence, Cybersecurity, etc.

More seriously, we will probably, alas, witness the same phenomenon as with Artificial Intelligence in the 2010 decade. The term AI had been heavily sold and it is still used by companies in need of funds or customers. I'm pretty sure we will see an Internet-connected can of beans with embedded artificial intelligence. So be ready for a flop of start-ups that will quantum wash whiter than white and that will succeed to attract poor informed investors, especially in seed capital.

Never forget that Quantum Computing is extremely complex, that it requires huge investments, that it needs to attract and to retain rare and expensive talents and that the first entrants have already filed a nice number of patents.

My humble opinion: Quantum Grail, if there is any, will be more at the level of manufacturing and selling shovels and jeans like in the Gold Rush.

Proof that this is not easy even at the application level: in 2018, Rigetti Computing offered \$1M, via its Quantum Advantage Prize contest, to reward the best proposal that can solve, using its Quantum Computing services in the Cloud, a *useful* problem (sic) *more efficiently, faster or cheaper* than a conventional computer. For Rigetti, the founder of the eponymous company, the question was no longer whether or not it was possible to make a quantum computer - there were already several - but to identify the *quantum advantage*.

Here is a list (updated to 2019) of some examples of quantum start-ups that seem interesting and promising:

- **1QBit**, Canadian quantum expertise society, offers a development kit (SDK) and interfaces (API) to its quantum computing platform that is independent of quantum computer technology type. The World Economic Forum has distinguished this company as Technology Pioneer in Quantum Computing.

- **Entropica Labs**, Singaporean company, builds an algorithmic platform specialized in bioinformatics, based on Quantum Computing and Artificial Intelligence. Its goal is to better model interactions at the molecular level.

- **GTN**, English company founded in 2016, develops computational models combining Artificial Intelligence and Quantum Computing to discover new drugs.

- **Muquans**, French company founded in 2011, designs and manufactures innovative quantum sensors.

- **OTI Lumionics,** Canadian company, researches new materials and designs new technologies for OLED screens using Artificial Intelligence and Quantum Computing.

- **ProteinQure**, Canadian company, designs and tests new protein-based drugs. It uses Quantum Computing to simulate how a protein folds in addition to more classical computations of molecular simulations on GPU and Artificial Intelligence.

- **QxBranch**, American company founded in 2014, specialized in forecasting analysis (price and market analysis, risk analysis, fraud, customer behavior) for the financial, pharmaceutical, insurance and media sectors.

- **Qulab**, American company specialized in automated molecular design for the chemical and pharmaceutical industries. The company is a partner of Rigetti Computing. It is constantly looking to optimize its Artificial Intelligence algorithms via the Cloud with the latest developments in Quantum Computing and specialized graphics cards (GPU).

- **QCWare**, American company founded in 2014, designs a development platform and algorithms independent of the quantum computer technology type. This abstraction layer (SDK and API) allows business customers to focus on solving business problems without worrying about the complexity of Quantum Computing. The platform is available via the Cloud.

- **Riverlane Research**, English company, uses Quantum Computing to discover and design new materials and medicines. The company has developed a virtual quantum computer that can test and execute chemistry-specific algorithms.

- **Solid State AI**, Canadian company, uses Quantum Computing and Artificial Intelligence to solve complex problems in predictive maintenance, optimization of production or yields and quality improvement in industrial processes.

- **Strangeworks**, American company, provides a pragmatic approach to quantum programming, regardless of the hardware.

- **Zapata Computing**, US company, Harvard spin-off in 2017, specializes in the design of quantum algorithms for the chemicals, finance, pharmaceutical, logistics and materials engineering sectors.

The main players, Microsoft, Google, IBM, Rigetti and D-Wave, have set up partnership programs with the most promising start-ups.

Two sectors sound attractive for a new venture:

- Companies specialized in the use of Quantum Computing in a specific field that requires specialized algorithms and business expertise (chemistry, biology, genetics, finance) ;

- Service providers that will train, certify (and propose to their customers) experts in Quantum Computing. VoltaNode is an example, with a comprehensive training and consulting services in Quantum Computing.

14.   CONCLUSION

At the end of my lectures, I regularly get the same question, "*What is the Killer Application of Quantum Computing?*". My answer always disappoints: "*None up to now. We are still looking*".

I am often asked another question, "*Will a quantum computer ever be able to simulate a human brain?*". You will hate my answer, necessarily quantum: "*Yes and No*".

Modeling, simulating and augmenting (replacing?) the human brain is one of the major projects of *transhumanism*. A project of this type already exists on a European scale, the "Human Brain Project", led by the Israeli neuroscientist Henry Markram and with an impressive budget of 1.2 billion euros. The first results are expected in 2024. This project has been very controversial within the European scientific community. Its scope has thus been reduced in its complexity. The main human brain (the cortex) has several billion neurons that each connects up to 10,000 other neurons, via dozens of different chemical pathways (ion channels) used by a dozen chemical messengers. In short, it's a complex system of at least 10,000 billion variables. It will probably be a good candidate for Quantum Computing around 2070!

It is also unlikely that people will have access to a quantum computer at home before fifty years at least, but we have seen that today it is possible to access to this technology via the Cloud.

In the early 2010s, Quantum Computer was still a theoretical view and most experts agreed that hundreds of thousands or millions of qubits should be needed to develop a usable quantum computer because of quantum errors.

It was also said that a quantum computer might be relevant only with a number of qubits greater than the number of qubits that a conventional computer could simulate.

Today, at the dawn of the 2020s, the paradigm has radically changed thanks to new hybrid algorithms that better identify and correct quantum errors. Using a quantum computer with only a few dozen qubits is already very interesting. Reaching from 80 to 100 qubits seems a possible and attainable goal in 2020. In 2019, Google has announced a 72-qubit system and Rigetti a 128-qubit by the end of 2019.

I'll end with this quote from D-Wave founder Jeremy Hilton:

"THE REVOLUTION OF QUANTUM COMPUTING WILL BE LIKELY DEEPER THAN CLASSICAL COMPUTING AND DIGITAL AGE, 50 YEARS AGO, AND WILL OCCUR QUICKER THAN EXPECTED".

15.   THE MATHEMATICS SHELTER

When I asked some friends and professional colleagues to proofread the very first draft version of this book, I got inevitably the same criticism, formulated differently according to the technical level of my interlocutors: it lacked proofs or mathematical explanations. The book was intended for the wider public in a spirit of popularization, so my bias had been to reduce the necessary knowledge in Mathematics to the bare minimum. I was told that a reader simply curious by nature would perhaps want to go further to really understand what is behind these so mysterious quantum phenomena.

I heard these criticisms and decided to include, in this last Chapter, for the most mathematical addicts of my readers, a brief mathematical introduction to Quantum Computing. However, I have voluntarily limited these few pages to the basic principles that should be understandable to anyone who has obtained a Degree.

Spoiler : You'd better read your courses of Linear Algebra.

Disclaimer : The following text applies only to qubits in an isolated system, which is not totally true in reality, but with quantum world you already know that everything is complex!

In the Quantum World, we work in a Hilbert space $\mathcal{H}$, which is a vector space on the complex numbers field $\mathbb{C}$ with a scalar product.

A complex number z can be written as:

$z = a + ib$ where a and b are real numbers and i an imaginary number such as $i^2 = -1$.

The **scalar product** (or dot product) is an algebraical operation which associates a complex number to two vectors in the field $\mathbb{C}$. It should not be confused with the vector product whose result is a vector and not a scalar. Consider u and v, two vectors. There are several notations to represent the scalar product, $u \cdot v, (u|v), \langle u|v \rangle, \langle u, v \rangle$, but in Quantum Mechanics, everybody uses $\langle u|v \rangle$.

If we switch to matrix notation, for example in $\mathbb{C}^4$:

$$U = \begin{bmatrix} x_1 \\ x_2 \\ x_3 \\ x_4 \end{bmatrix}, V = \begin{bmatrix} y_1 \\ y_2 \\ y_3 \\ y_4 \end{bmatrix}, \qquad x_n, y_n \in \mathbb{C}$$

$$\langle u|v \rangle = {}^tUV = \begin{bmatrix} x_1 & x_2 & x_3 & x_4 \end{bmatrix} \begin{bmatrix} y_1 \\ y_2 \\ y_3 \\ y_4 \end{bmatrix}$$

$$= x_1 y_1 + x_2 y_2 + x_3 y_3 + x_4 y_4$$

With ${}^tU$ which is the transpose matrix of U and ${}^tUV$ the matrix product.

QUBIT IN ALL STATES

A qubit has a quantum state that is a probabilistic distribution. By using the notation specific to the quantum universe (Dirac notation), we can write this quantum state in the form of a column vector $|\psi\rangle$, called *ket* (pronounce « ket psi »), with $a_0, a_1 \in \mathbb{C}$. This is the famous vector of the spherical representation that starts from the center and can point to any point in the sphere. So, for a qubit, the Hilbert space is $\mathbb{C}^2$.

$$|\psi\rangle = \begin{bmatrix} a_0 \\ a_1 \end{bmatrix}$$

As we know that in probabilities, the sum of the probabilities is always equal to one, we can also write that:

$$\sqrt{|a_0|^2 + |a_1|^2} = 1$$

For those of my readers who remember some chunks of their Mathematics courses, you can decompose a vector into a canonical basis. The quantum canonical basis would then be, with Dirac's notation:

$$|0\rangle = \begin{bmatrix} 1 \\ 0 \end{bmatrix}, \qquad |1\rangle = \begin{bmatrix} 0 \\ 1 \end{bmatrix}$$

which are two specific qubits. Here is the decomposition of the *ket* into the canonical basis:

$$|\psi\rangle = \begin{bmatrix} a_0 \\ a_1 \end{bmatrix} = a_0 \begin{bmatrix} 1 \\ 0 \end{bmatrix} + a_1 \begin{bmatrix} 0 \\ 1 \end{bmatrix} = a_0|0\rangle + a_1|1\rangle$$

We truly get a superposition, with a result of 0 with a probability of $|a_0|^2$ and a result of 1 with a probability of $|a_1|^2$.

In Quantum Mechanics, there is another important vector, $\langle\psi|$, the transpose and complex conjugate vector of $|\psi\rangle$, (Hermitian conjugate, for purists) called *bra*, (pronounce « bra psi »).

You can write the scalar product of two vectors $|\psi\rangle$ and $|\phi\rangle$ as: $\langle\phi|\psi\rangle$. Physicist's nice word game: it's called a *bracket*!

Consider 2 qubits. The associated Hilbert space is $\mathbb{C}^2 \otimes \mathbb{C}^2$. Since $\mathbb{C}^2 \otimes \mathbb{C}^2$ is isomorphic to $\mathbb{C}^4$, it's possible to decompose the 2-qubit state with the corresponding canonical basis:

$$|\psi\rangle = a_{00}|0,0\rangle + a_{01}|0,1\rangle + a_{10}|1,0\rangle + a_{11}|1,1\rangle$$

With $|0,0\rangle = |0\rangle\otimes|0\rangle$, ctc.

And the canonical basis is:

$$|0,0\rangle = \begin{bmatrix} 1 \\ 0 \\ 0 \\ 0 \end{bmatrix}, |0,1\rangle = \begin{bmatrix} 0 \\ 1 \\ 0 \\ 0 \end{bmatrix}, |1,0\rangle = \begin{bmatrix} 0 \\ 0 \\ 1 \\ 0 \end{bmatrix}, |1,1\rangle = \begin{bmatrix} 0 \\ 0 \\ 0 \\ 1 \end{bmatrix}$$

You can easily generalize to a n-qubit system.

By the way, it will become a little more complex, so feel free to reread the previous lines so that you master the notation and concepts.

We will now move on to a $2n$-dimensional Hilbert space, to represent the state of a system of n qubits.

We note $|i\rangle$, with $i = 0$ to $2n\text{-}1$, an orthonormal basis of this space.

We can then decompose the state vector as follows:

$$|\psi\rangle = \sum_{i=0}^{2n-1} a_i|i\rangle$$

with $a_i = \langle i|\psi\rangle$.

If $n = 1$, the canonical decomposition is:

$$|\psi\rangle = \begin{bmatrix} a_0 \\ a_1 \end{bmatrix} = a_0 \begin{bmatrix} 1 \\ 0 \end{bmatrix} + a_1 \begin{bmatrix} 0 \\ 1 \end{bmatrix} = a_0|0\rangle + a_1|1\rangle$$

Let's try to understand what happens when calculating $a_i = \langle i|\psi\rangle$.

In fact, it is like projecting $|\psi\rangle$ on the vectors of the orthonormal basis. Basically, imagine a two-dimensional space, the plane of a sheet of paper, where you draw two perpendicular (orthogonal) axes, abscissa and ordinate. To position a point on the sheet, you can draw it at the intersection of its coordinates of x and y. If you draw a line between the origin (the intersection of the two coordinate axes) and this point, you get a vector. The values x and y are its projections on the vectors of the base (the two axes of orthogonal coordinates).

So we have:

$$|\psi\rangle = \sum_{i=0}^{2n-1} |i\rangle\langle i|\psi\rangle$$

We then identify $|i\rangle\langle i|$ as a **projector** of $|\psi\rangle$ on the basis vector $|i\rangle$. Afterwards, it will be noted P_i.

With these few concepts of quantum mathematics, let's get to the reality of our qubits.

If we consider an electron, we said that its quantum state was represented by its spin. A spin ½ (2-level system) can be described in the Bloch Sphere like the following:

$$\cos\frac{\theta}{2}|0\rangle + e^{-i\phi} \sin\frac{\theta}{2}|1\rangle$$

Knowing that: $0 \leq \theta \leq \pi$ et $0 \leq \phi \leq 2\pi$.

Note that in the Bloch Sphere: $|0\rangle \cong (0,0,1)$, $|1\rangle \cong (0,0,-1)$

If we switch to $\mathbb{R}^3$:

$$\begin{aligned} x &= \sin\theta * \cos\phi \\ y &= \sin\theta * \sin\phi \\ z &= \cos\theta \end{aligned}$$

We have similar equations for the polarization of photons.

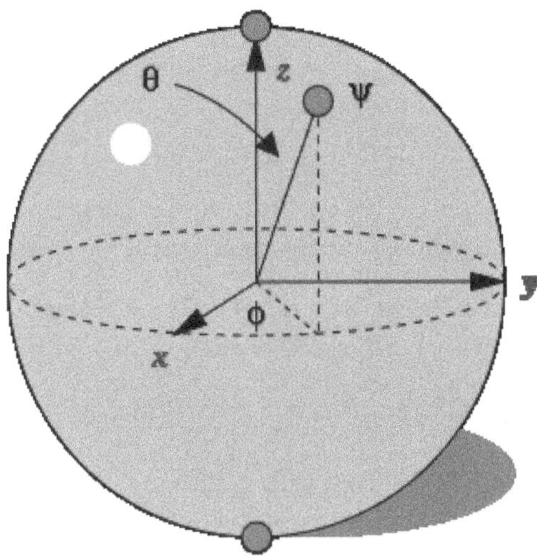

Figure 16: Quantum State in the Bloch Sphere

QUBITS & SPIN

In Quantum Mechanics, the elementary particles that make up the matter around us are called **fermions**. Protons, neutrons and electrons are fermions.

I have spoken several times about the spin of a particle. The spin describes, among other things, the number of rotations needed for a particle to return to its initial state.

All fermions have a spin of 1/2. That means that a double rotation (ie 720°) must be made to return to the initial configuration of the particle, which is rather difficult to explain in classical physics.

It is possible to describe and write this state by the linear combination of two **eigenstates** called spin up $|\uparrow\rangle$ and spin down $|\downarrow\rangle$.

MEASURE ET QUANTUM COLLAPSE

We now come to one of the fundamental principles of Quantum Physics: the **measurement** of a state. It is also one of the most difficult specificities for architects of these new computers.

If we measure 3 qubits, we get 3 bits whose probability is given by the square of the magnitude of the corresponding coefficient: for example the probability of measuring '000' $= |a_0|^2$, the probability of measuring '001' $= |a_1|^2$, etc.

So, if we measure a quantum state $(a_0,a_1,a_2,a_3,a_4,a_5,a_6,a_7)$, we get a classical probability distribution:

$$(|a_0|^2, |a_1|^2, |a_2|^2, |a_3|^2, |a_4|^2, |a_5|^2, |a_6|^2, |a_7|^2)$$

The quantum state is said to have *collapsed* or has been reduced to a classical (non-quantum) state because of the measurement.

Imagine a system or a device that can measure a quantum state $|\psi\rangle$. This system is modeled by a set of projectors P_i.

So we can write that once the measurement is done, the state changes to $|\phi\rangle$:

$$|\phi\rangle = \frac{P_i|\psi\rangle}{\|P_i|\psi\rangle\|}$$

Consequently, the state $|\phi\rangle$ is actually random and not predictive! The measurement must be repeated several times to obtain a probability of obtaining a certain result.

Even if a qubit can exist in an arbitrary superposition state, measuring its state will always give one of its two eigenstates, $|0\rangle$ or $|1\rangle$, which is reduced to one bit.

This means that during its measurement, the qubit somehow loses its quantum character and that this measurement is irreversible (which poses quite a lot of problems in the design of a quantum computer and algorithms).

ENTANGLEMENT

Let's move on to a slightly more complex concept, the entanglement of two qubits.

One more time, Mathematics explain this paradox.

Consider two qubits and arbitrarily select that their quantum state, a bit peculiar, is the following:

$$|\psi\rangle = |0,0\rangle + |1,1\rangle$$

It is impossible to mathematically decompose this state into one form of each considered state separately. Indeed, there is no (a_0,a_1,a_2,a_3) such as:

$$|0,0\rangle + |1,1\rangle = (a_0|0\rangle + a_1|1\rangle) \otimes (a_2|0\rangle + a_3|1\rangle)$$

HOLEVO'S THEOREM

Let me provide some additional information about the famous Holevo's Theorem. This concept is often poorly explained and needs some demystification without going too much into the mathematical demonstration that is somehow difficult.

I have often read or heard about the Holevo's Theorem (it is also commonly referred to as *Holevo's Limit*), that n qubits might not *encode* more than n classical bits. It's wrong.

I myself used the term *'carry'* in the book to simplify the first reading. This term is not correct either.

Indeed, thanks to the principle of superposition, it is possible to code, to *carry*, a very large amount of conventional binary information on a system of n qubits. But, what proves Holevo's Theorem is that it is possible to find or access only a maximum of n bits.

To end up destabilizing the most diligent reader, may I add that it takes 2^n-1 complex numbers to encode the qubits necessary to represent n bits. Decidedly, Quantum Computing is really weird!

CLASSICAL LOGIC AND QUANTUM LOGIC

Long before quantum computers became a reality, researchers worked on the possibility of creating quantum algorithms.

All current classical computers are based on the binary logic theory. The question had been whether a quantum equivalence was possible. The answer is yes.

Basically, it was demonstrated, from the works of Turing [12] and Church [13] in 1936, that it was possible to translate any mathematical function into a set of simple binary functions, called **gates**.

Current computing science and especially microprocessors have been designed and built around this concept.

Three simple binary gates (called also *operators*) were identified: two with two entries - AND and OR - and one with an entry, NOT.

In binary logic, binary operators are often described by their *truth table*, which is very easy to read. If we call a_1 and a_2 the input binary data, the truth tables are written as follows:

A_1	A_2	A_1 AND A_2
0	0	0
0	1	0
1	0	0
1	1	1

A_1	A_2	A_1 OR A_2
0	0	0
0	1	1
1	0	1
1	1	1

A_1	NOT A_1
0	1
1	0

These three operators are *universal*.

It is already interesting and surprising to note that any calculation on any real or complex number (as soon as decomposed into a binary number) can be expressed by a combination of these three universal binary operators.

The NOT operator is also represented as follows in graph theory (we will come back to it in quantum logic):

$$a_1 \quad \longmapsto\!\!\oplus\!\!\longmapsto \quad \text{NOT } a_1$$

It is nevertheless possible to go further into simplification by introducing a second type of binary operators: NAND and NOR.

$$a_1 \text{ NAND } a_2 = \text{NOT } (a_1 \text{ AND } a_2)$$

$$a_1 \text{ NOR } a_2 = \text{NOT } (a_1 \text{ OR } a_2).$$

The truth tables are :

116

A_1	A_2	A_1 NAND A_2
0	0	1
0	1	1
1	0	1
1	1	0

A_1	A_2	A_1 NOR A_2
0	0	1
0	1	0
1	0	0
1	1	0

Remarkably, it is shown that any calculation can be reduced to a combination of NAND (operator) only (or NOR only) gates. In just a few decades, the NAND gate has become the queen of microprocessors. It is therefore sufficient for microprocessor vendors to optimize and master the manufacturing of the NAND gate.

If the operator is not reversible, this means that information has been lost since we cannot go back to the original data. However, the laws of fundamental physics dictate that no loss of information is possible without dissipation of energy. This means that even with the best technology and circuit design, there will always be wasted energy that needs to be dissipated. The energy level per NAND gate may seem negligible but if you multiply it by the number of gates (dozens of millions) in a modern microprocessor, this becomes an important variable to take into account.

Chip manufacturers have therefore researched *reversible* operators that do not dissipate energy due to the loss of information.

The NOT operator is reversible because it is possible to find the input data from the single result. You just need to apply the operator one more time to himself.

The operators AND, OR, NAND and NOR are not reversible because they provide a single result while there are two entries. It is obviously impossible to find the two entries from the single result.

This notion of reversibility has important consequences in information theory (entropy) and physics (energy consumed). The researchers have therefore proposed new operators such as CNOT (or XOR) which is a NOT controlled by a bit.

A_1	A_2	A_1 CNOT A_2
0	0	0
0	1	1
1	0	1
1	1	0

The graph representation of the operator CNOT is:

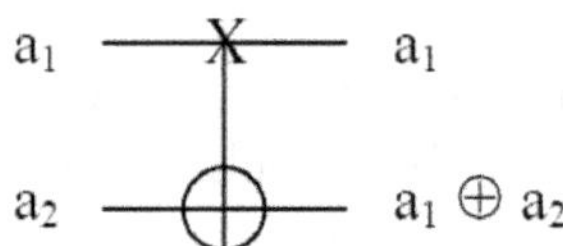

It is reversible but it is not universal.

The mathematician Toffoli proved in 1981 [14] that a similar operator with three entries is actually universal: the CCNOT (we also note it T) whose representation is:

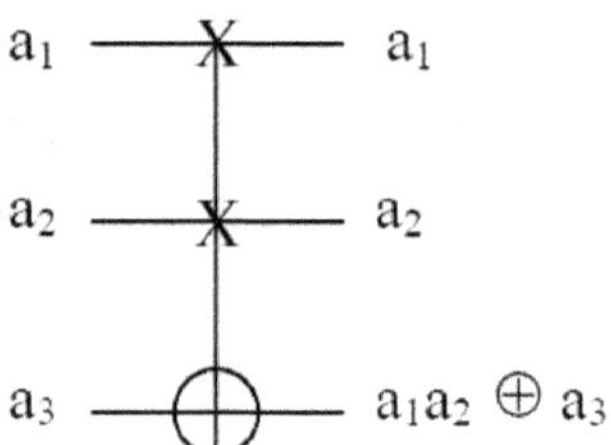

The truth table is :

A₁	A₂	A₃	A₁,A₂ CCNOT A₃
0	0	0	0
0	0	1	1
0	1	0	0
0	1	1	1
1	0	0	0
1	0	1	1
1	1	0	1
1	1	1	0

This operator applies a NOT to the 3rd bit if the first two bits are 1.

Another interesting operator is SWAP which has two representations:

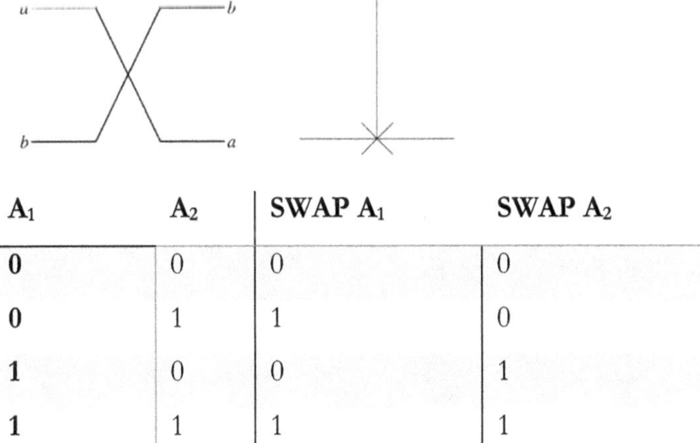

A₁	A₂	SWAP A₁	SWAP A₂
0	0	0	0
0	1	1	0
1	0	0	1
1	1	1	1

These few explanations in binary logic were necessary to better understand what happens in quantum logic.

In 1985, the mathematician Deutsch published a seminal article [15] on the existence of the quantum analogy of the famous Turing machine. He thus demonstrated that any problem that can be simulated in a classical way can also be simulated in a quantum way. The basic operator, invertible, is the unitary matrix with conservation of the norm.

A unitary matrix in a Hermitian vector space is a bit like an orthogonal matrix in a Euclidean vector space. Any unitary matrix product is also unitary (and therefore invertible).

The evolution of a quantum state over the time is a unitary matrix U, invertible, applied to the initial state:

$$|\psi(t)\rangle = U|\psi(0)\rangle$$

Now let's introduce the Pauli Matrices that can decompose an elementary qubit.

$$I = \begin{bmatrix} 1 & 0 \\ 0 & 1 \end{bmatrix}, \quad X = \begin{bmatrix} 0 & 1 \\ 1 & 0 \end{bmatrix}, \quad Y = \begin{bmatrix} 0 & -i \\ i & 0 \end{bmatrix}, \quad Z = \begin{bmatrix} 1 & 0 \\ 0 & -1 \end{bmatrix}$$

Note that all invertible (logical) Boolean operators can be expressed as a unitary transformation.

We can already translate NOT and CNOT operators into quantum logic, as unitary matrices, which are capable of transforming states into superposition:

$$U_{NOT} = \begin{bmatrix} 0 & 1 \\ 1 & 0 \end{bmatrix} \quad U_{CNOT} = \begin{bmatrix} 1 & 0 & 0 & 0 \\ 0 & 1 & 0 & 0 \\ 0 & 0 & 0 & 1 \\ 0 & 0 & 1 & 0 \end{bmatrix} \quad U_{SWAP} = \begin{bmatrix} 1 & 0 & 0 & 0 \\ 0 & 0 & 1 & 0 \\ 0 & 1 & 0 & 0 \\ 0 & 0 & 0 & 1 \end{bmatrix}$$

Note that the Pauli Matrix X seems equivalent to a NOT gate, which is not exactly true but the proof is outside the scope of this book.

Another fundamental and very useful operator is the Hadamard operator, which can create a superposition from an eigenstate. It can be written as follows:

$$U_H = \frac{1}{\sqrt{2}} \begin{bmatrix} 1 & 1 \\ 1 & -1 \end{bmatrix}$$

Its representation is:

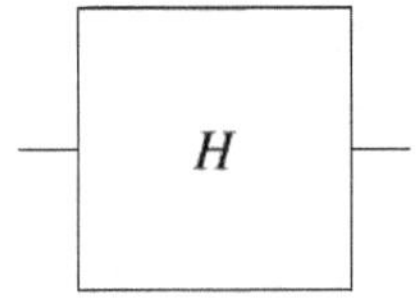

In my opinion, this is the most important quantum operator because it allows to generate the multiple quantum states necessary to take advantage of the features of Quantum Computing. If we have a system of n qubits that is initialized in the state $|0\rangle$ and if the Hadamard operator is applied to each qubit, the result is a superposition of n qubits with 2^n eigenstates.

The CNOT operator has three very interesting features.

First, it can perform a measurement on a qubit because it can clone the eigenstates of a qubit (which are the only cloneable states, remember it):

If a is $|0\rangle$ or $|1\rangle$, then:

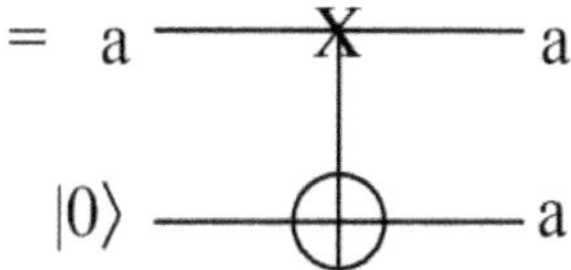

Then, if the qubit is not in one of its eigenstates but on the contrary in a superposition state (and thus non-cloneable), the CNOT operator can generate a state of entanglement as one sees it on the diagram below:

This operator, like in classical logic, can also perform error corrections, which is essential in Quantum Computing.

There are other operators : SWAP operator (denoted S) and a particular operator, called Fredkin (denoted F) which is a SWAP operator controlled by a third qubit.

To perform all possible transformations on the qubits, it is necessary to have rotation and phase change operators. These operators have the following structure (with $0 \leq \theta \leq 2\pi$) :

$$\begin{bmatrix} \cos\theta & \sin\theta \\ -\sin\theta & \cos\theta \end{bmatrix} , \quad \begin{bmatrix} e^{i\theta} & 0 \\ 0 & e^{-i\theta} \end{bmatrix}$$

Your First Quantum Circuit

As your first quantum circuit, I propose we build a qubit adder. This function, even simple, requires some design thinking without forgetting the constraints of Quantum Computing.

This adder should accept two qubits $|x\rangle$ and $|y\rangle$ as entries. It should manage the carry $|c\rangle$ from upstream (never forget computation is achieved at one-bit resolution!). The sum of the two qubits will be $|s\rangle$ and the downstream carry $|c'\rangle$.

The diagram is the following:

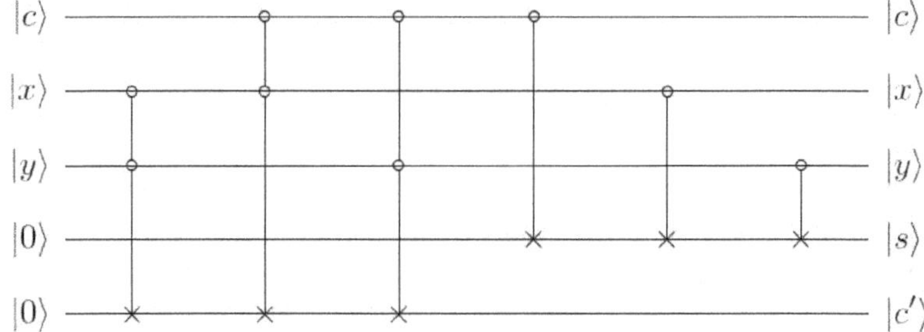

So, this adder uses CNOT and CCNOT gates (called Toffoli, also called T, the most used notation).

Performing the matrix calculations corresponding to this adder is a good exercise for checking your full understanding of the concepts behind.

REFERENCES

[1] M. A. Nielsen and I. L. Chuang, Quantum Computation and Quantum Information, Cambridge University Press, 2000.

[2] P. Dirac, The Principles of Quantum Mechanics, Oxford University Press, 1930.

[3] J. v. Neumann, Mathematische Grundlagen der Quantenmechanik, Julius Springer, 1932.

[4] C. H. Bennett and G. Brassard, "Teleporting an Unknown Quantum State via Dual Classical and Einstein–Podolsky–Rosen Channels," *Physical Review Letters,* vol. 70, no. 13, pp. 1895-1899, 1993.

[5] Y. S. Chang, J. Lee et Y. S. Jung, «Are technology improvement rates of knowledge industries following Moore's law? An empirical study of microprocessor, mobile cellular, and genome sequencing technologies,» *International Journal of Technology Management,,* vol. 78, n° %13, pp. 182-207, 2018.

[6] A. S. Holevo, «Bounds for the quantity of information transmitted by a quantum communication channel,» *Problems of Information Transmission,* vol. 9, pp. 177-183, 1973.

[7] R. S. Ingarden, «Quantum Information Theory,» *Reports on Mathematical Physics,* vol. 10, p. 43–72, 1976.

[8] R. Feynman, «Simulating Physics with Computers,» *Internationl Journal of Theorical Physics,* vol. 21, n° %16/7, pp. 467-488, 1982.

[9] C. H. Bennett et G. Brassard, «Quantum Cryptography, Public Ley Distribution and Coin Tossing,» chez *International Conference on Computers, Systems & Signal Processing*, Bangalore, India, 1984.

[10] A. Harrow, A. Hassidim and S. Lloyd, "Quantum algorithm for solving linear systems of equations," *Phys. Rev. Lett.,* vol. 15, 2009.

[11] C. Beigbeder et C. Jurczak, «Les technologies quantiques sont en passe de révolutionner des pans entiers de l'économie,» *Le Monde,* 26 Mars 2019.

[12] A. Turing, «On computable numbers with an application to the Entscheidungs-problem,» *London Mathematics Society,* vol. Ser. 2, pp. 230-65, 1936.

[13] A. Church, «An unsolvable problem of elementary number theory,» *American Journal of Mathematics,* vol. 58, pp. 345-63, 1936.

[14] T. Toffoli, «Reversible Computing,» MIT Lab, 1980.

[15] D. Deutsch, «Quantum theory, the Church-Turing principle and the universal quantum computer,» chez *Proceedings Royal Society London,* 97-117, 1985.

[16] D. R. Stinson, Cryptography: Theory and Practice, Chapman and Hall/CRC, 2005.

[17] D. P. DiVicenzo, "The Physical Implementation of Quantum Computation," *Fortschritte der Physik,* vol. 48, no. 9-11, pp. 771-783, 2000.

ABOUT THE AUTHOR

Franck Franchin is a swiss-french expert in cybersecurity and information technology. Professor in Masters and instructor in companies, he likes to popularize new technologies such as Artificial Intelligence, Quantum Computing or Cryptography. He founded several start-ups in cryptography and digital content distribution. During his career, he has also been responsible for innovation and cybersecurity at Orange, Vivendi and Thales. He graduated of a MBA from ESCP, a Master's degree in Computer Science from CentraleSupélec and a Master's degree in Electronics from ENSEEIHT.

www.ingramcontent.com/pod-product-compliance
Lightning Source LLC
LaVergne TN
LVHW010346200726
843507LV00010B/1665